Praise for *Automating Data Quality Monitoring*

This book expertly lays out the entire data quality lifecycle from rules definitions and machine learning to scaling and alert fatigue. A canonical resource.

—*Chris Riccomini, Author of* The Missing README: A Guide for the New Software Engineer

Data quality has become an imperative—it can be the difference between creating value or eroding trust. This book represents a step change in how to think about and pragmatically approach this critical topic.

—*Chris Mazzei, Adjunct Professor of Strategy and AI at Cornell and NYU Former Global Vice Chair Strategy, Data and Analytics, EY*

Excellent overview of practical monitoring solutions powered by machine learning and adapted to the maturity of your modern data stack. You don't have to earn your data scars—you can just read this book.

—*Monica Rogati, Independent Data Science Advisor*

In an era where AI is reshaping enterprises, this book offers a powerful roadmap for ensuring foundational data quality, a must-read for forward-thinking data leaders.

—*Chen Peng, VP and Head of Data at Faire*

This book covers everything from ROI to GenAI to answer all your questions about managing data quality in business.

—*Auren Hoffman, CEO of Safegraph and Host of the World of DaaS Podcast*

In the next age of Generative AI and ML, models will soon be powered by every bit of data in your data ecosystem. The novel approach proposed in this book to scale data quality monitoring using ML is compelling. At Discover, we have achieved solid ROI using this approach.

—*Keith Toney, EVP, President, Credit and Decision Management at Discover Financial Services*

A must-read for professionals seeking to unlock the full potential of their data through the application of machine learning techniques.

—*Gilad Lotan, Head of Data Science and Analytics at BuzzFeed Inc.*

Automating Data Quality Monitoring

Monitoring

Scaling Beyond Rules with Machine Learning

Jeremy Stanley and Paige Schwartz

Beijing • Boston • Farnham • Sebastopol • Tokyo

Automating Data Quality Monitoring

by Jeremy Stanley and Paige Schwartz

Published by O'Reilly Media, Inc., 1005 Gravenstein Highway North, Sebastopol, CA 95472.

O'Reilly books may be purchased for educational, business, or sales promotional use. Online editions are also available for most titles (*http://oreilly.com*). For more information, contact our corporate/institutional sales department: 800-998-9938 or *corporate@oreilly.com*.

Acquisitions Editor: Aaron Black	**Indexer:** Ellen Troutman-Zaig
Development Editor: Gary O'Brien	**Interior Designer:** David Futato
Production Editor: Jonathon Owen	**Cover Designer:** Karen Montgomery
Copyeditor: nSight, Inc.	**Illustrator:** Kate Dullea
Proofreader: Krsta Technology Solutions	

January 2024:   First Edition

Revision History for the First Edition
2024-01-09:   First Release

See *http://oreilly.com/catalog/errata.csp?isbn=9781098145934* for release details.

978-1-098-14593-4

[LSI]

Table of Contents

Foreword

A quick question for you: How can you tell a data scientist who's actually built things in production from someone who's just played with data? Answer: They've been absolutely burned by data quality. Anybody who's really deployed data has not just one scar, but lashes across their entire body from this problem.

Here's a typical day in the life of a data science team. A senior executive sees something weird on a dashboard in the morning, asks if the number is right, and then the data team sprints for the next 4 hours to figure out the answer. They finally track down the engineer who forgot to add the right tracking mechanism. But now it's past noon and the team hasn't even gotten to their long list of to-dos for the day! Coming out of firefighting mode, it's hard to make forward progress on anything interesting.

Another way of saying this is that we always let the urgent get in the way of the important. More dangerous is that we undermine trust in the data. The data science teams end up playing defense rather than offense.

I've seen this firsthand so many times. At the beginning of the COVID-19 pandemic, I was asked to help the state of California with understanding the potential impact of the disease. It was an all-hands-on-deck moment, and we had access to incredible resources and data sets. Yet we were still questioning basic numbers on dashboards like the number of ICU beds available or how much protective gear was remaining at a given hospital. To track down issues in the pipeline, we had to do the equivalent of using `printf` statements to debug where the data had gone wrong. Unfortunately, we didn't have a way of running diagnostics to answer very simple questions that carried enormous ramifications.

Dashboards and decision making are just scratching the surface—what about AI, and generative AI in particular? With all the excitement, it sometimes seems like we're forgetting the foundations and how big of an impact data quality has; we can't inspect and debug AI systems like typical software. While the opportunities here are great, so are the risks, and operating black-box models without data quality control is a scary prospect.

The fact that data scientists and engineers recognize these problems is an accomplishment in and of itself, because it means we have evolved to the next phase of data utilization. The first phase was the democratization of data. Now we're using the data! And with the use of data comes great responsibility, and we need the data teams to be in better control of their destiny. The analogy is akin to the tools engineers have like observability platforms, on-call systems, QA environments, DevOps tooling, etc. Data practitioners should have the necessary tooling that lets them get out ahead of the root cause of data issues. That's what this book is about.

To write a really good technical book, you need to have lived it. Jeremy has the scars that come from working on data quality not just at one organization, but with many teams and stakeholders across different sectors and dimensions. In addition, he's the founder of a company in the space (full disclosure that I am also an investor). They understand the issues up and down the stack, including all the cultural, political, and technical dynamics. The people who will solve data observability are those with unbelievable empathy for the problems, and that's what you will find here.

My advice to readers: Don't feel like you have to read this book straight through on the first go. Instead, skim through it and get the lay of the land. It's just like a dataset. You play with it, see what's there and what interests you, and then go deeper over time. You can apply this book in pieces, digest it, and refer to it whenever you're facing a specific problem. I have no doubt you'll want to come back to these pages again and again.

— DJ Patil, PhD
General Partner, GreatPoint Ventures
Former US Chief Data Scientist

Preface

Most companies, when they achieve sufficient size and scale, reach a point when they begin to question whether their data is trustworthy. They observe numbers on dashboards that can't possibly be accurate; out of the blue, machine learning models begin performing poorly in production. The phrase "garbage in, garbage out" starts to circulate internally—referring to the problem of building products and features using data that may contain corruptions, missing segments, and other inaccuracies.

When trust in the company's data starts to degrade—or perhaps has never existed in the first place—it's essential to address this issue head-on. Data quality isn't something that magically improves as a company continues to grow; in fact, it will only get worse due to increased complexity. Data quality, like software quality, needs to be continually monitored so that problems are fixed quickly as they arise.

Many organizations are on board with this idea in theory but struggle to implement data quality monitoring in practice, at enterprise scale. When Jeremy and Elliott founded Anomalo in 2018, it was because of firsthand experience with these struggles, resulting in a realization that existing approaches to data quality monitoring weren't serving the needs of modern businesses.

Writing rules to check every piece of business logic that must be met for every table and every column might have worked when companies maintained just a few small, well-controlled tables, but with current data volumes, it feels like trying to boil the ocean. Tracking KPIs can give you an important signal about data quality, and so can observing basic metadata such as whether data arrives on time—but still, the coverage is insufficient, and you won't have a way to catch all the issues you didn't think to look for.

That's why we're so excited about the approach we'll share in this book: automating data quality monitoring with machine learning. ML is an incredibly powerful tool that's shaping innovation everywhere, and the data quality space is no different. In this book, we share knowledge from five years of building an ML-powered data quality monitoring platform that's used by enterprise customers in a wide variety of industries. These chapters contain the most cutting-edge techniques we know—whether we're talking about how to develop an unsupervised model to detect issues in your data, how to benchmark and tune that model, or how to ensure that your notifications are not too noisy.

If you decide to invest in this technology, it most likely won't be a moment too soon. Data is driving the latest iteration of technological change through better decisions, automation, and generative AI. The quality of your data ultimately affects how impactful your organization's products and services will be in this new, and ever-shifting, landscape. And when businesses can build better technology, we all feel the benefits of the collective innovation—whether that's economic, societal, or even personal impact.

So, improve your data quality, and you might just save the world? Maybe that's a bit of an exaggeration. But we do think that you'll learn a thing or two from this book, and hopefully have fun along the way.

We'll close with this: data quality is an ongoing journey. There is a great deal of innovation happening in the space right now, and we expect more innovation to come. Perhaps as the reader, you'll even take the techniques in this book a step further—this is our hope, and if that's the case, we would love to hear from you. You can contact the authors directly at *automating.data.quality.monitoring@anomalo.com*.

Who Should Use This Book

We've written this book with three main audiences in mind.

The first is the chief data and analytics officer (CDAO) or VP of data. As someone responsible for your organization's data at the highest level, this entire book is for you—but you may be most interested in Chapters 1, 2, and 3, where we clearly explain why you should care about automating data quality monitoring at your organization and walk through how to assess the ROI of an automated data quality monitoring platform. Chapter 8 is also especially relevant, as it discusses how to track and improve data quality over time.

The second audience for this book is the head of data governance. In this or similar roles, you're likely the person most directly accountable for managing data quality at your organization. While the entire book should be of great value to you, we believe that the chapters on automation, Chapters 1, 2, and 3, as well as Chapters 7 and 8 on integrations and operations, will be especially useful.

Our third audience is the data practitioner. Whether you're a data scientist, analyst, or data engineer, your job depends on data quality, and the monitoring tools you use will have a significant impact on your day-to-day. Those building or operating a data quality monitoring platform should focus especially on Chapters 4 through 7, where we cover how to develop a model, design notifications, and integrate the platform with your data ecosystem.

Conventions Used in This Book

The following typographical conventions are used in this book:

Italic
> Indicates new terms, URLs, email addresses, filenames, and file extensions.

`Constant width`
> Used for program listings, as well as within paragraphs to refer to program elements such as variable or function names, databases, data types, environment variables, statements, and keywords.

 This element signifies a tip or suggestion.

 This element signifies a general note.

 This element indicates a warning or caution.

O'Reilly Online Learning

O'REILLY® For more than 40 years, *O'Reilly Media* has provided technology and business training, knowledge, and insight to help companies succeed.

Our unique network of experts and innovators share their knowledge and expertise through books, articles, and our online learning platform. O'Reilly's online learning platform gives you on-demand access to live training courses, in-depth learning paths, interactive coding environments, and a vast collection of text and video from O'Reilly and 200+ other publishers. For more information, visit *https://oreilly.com*.

How to Contact Us

Please address comments and questions concerning this book to the publisher:

O'Reilly Media, Inc.
1005 Gravenstein Highway North
Sebastopol, CA 95472
800-889-8969 (in the United States or Canada)
707-829-7019 (international or local)
707-829-0104 (fax)
support@oreilly.com
https://www.oreilly.com/about/contact.html

We have a web page for this book, where we list errata, examples, and any additional information. You can access this page at *https://oreil.ly/automating-data-quality*.

For news and information about our books and courses, visit *https://oreilly.com*.

Find us on LinkedIn: *https://linkedin.com/company/oreilly-media*

Follow us on Twitter: *https://twitter.com/oreillymedia*

Watch us on YouTube: *https://youtube.com/oreillymedia*

Acknowledgments

This book would not have been possible without contributions from a great number of people. Anomalo's CEO and cofounder, Elliot Shmukler, shared in the creation and discovery of many of the innovations in this book and has been an indispensable reviewer. Vicky Andonova, a founding team member of Anomalo and our Manager of Applied Machine Learning also developed and refined many of the ideas in this book. Other internal reviewers from Anomalo include Anthony Lee, Amy Reams, Erick Peirson, John Joo, Lucy Vallejo-Anderson, Taly Kanfi, and Tristen Cross, who shared excellent inputs and feedback. This book would not have been possible without all the Anomollamas (many not mentioned here) who bring their creativity and insight to develop our platform and help our customers every day. Thank you.

Other advisors and friends we'd like to thank include: Monica Rogati, a prominent data science advisor; Daniele Perito, cofounder of Faire, who coined the term *data scars*; Prakash Jaganathan, Senior Director of Enterprise Data Platforms at Discover, for providing an early review and allowing us to link to his excellent ROI case study; the team at Chick-fil-A for providing invaluable insight into their platform onboarding process; DJ Patil for promoting our early release; Josh Wills for his humor and insights; and Josie Stanley for sharing her artistic talents.

We would like to extend a big thanks to the team at O'Reilly, including our incredible editor Gary O'Brien and our book production and management team: Aaron Black, Jonathon Owen, Elizabeth Faerm, Carol Keller, Kristen Brown, Lisa LaRew, Patrick McGrath, and Phil Garzoli. We'd also like to thank our O'Reilly technical reviewers, Oscar Quintana, Pier Paolo Ippolito, Shubham Piyushbhai Patel, and Wayne Yaddow, for bringing their industry expertise and external perspectives to the book and sharing important comments and questions that improved the content.

## CHAPTER 1

The Data Quality Imperative

In March 2022, Equifax was migrating its data from on-premises systems to a new cloud infrastructure, a notoriously tricky process. Somewhere along the way, an error was introduced (*https://oreil.ly/5QLPJ*) impacting how credit scores were calculated. Roughly 12% of all the company's credit score data was affected, and hundreds of thousands of people ended up with scores that were off by 25 points or more (*https://oreil.ly/l5Zw8*). Unaware of the error, lending institutions that consumed Equifax's data altered the rates they offered custofmers and even rejected loan and mortgage applications that should have been approved.

Unfortunately, this isn't the only data quality mess that's made the news recently:

- In 2020, a data error (*https://oreil.ly/LzkkB*) caused the loss of nearly 16,000 positive COVID-19 test results in the United Kingdom, possibly resulting in 50,000 people not being told to self-isolate.

- So-called airline "mistake fares," (*https://oreil.ly/GDR8a*) which are sometimes unintentionally discounted by more than 90%, have forced airlines to either lose money or injure their reputations by failing to honor (*https://oreil.ly/bWrv2*) these "glitch prices."

- Facebook provided a dataset (*https://oreil.ly/h25bk*) to a group of social scientists that left out half of all its US users, affecting the findings in academic work studying the impact of social media on elections and democracy.

- The video game company Unity lost $110 million (*https://oreil.ly/sy8OB*) on their AI advertising system after ingesting bad training data from a third party.

These news stories show the impact that particularly bad data quality issues can have—but that's not the whole picture. The vast majority of data quality issues are never caught and are sneakily destroying value for companies as you read this. Of those that are caught, few are publicly disclosed.

Here are two anecdotes you might find relatable if you've ever worked on a data team:

- One day, one of the product dashboards of a large tech company indicated a sudden drop in net promoter score (NPS) survey results. This most likely meant that customers were frustrated about a change in the product, so it set off alarm bells up and down the organization. Senior leadership became involved, and a task force was created. Engineers and analysts evaluated every code change from the past month and combed through all their user data to figure out what could have caused the plummeting scores.

  The root cause was finally uncovered by the data scientist analyzing the NPS data. In their analysis, they discovered that any scores of 9 or 10 (out of 10) had stopped appearing entirely in the latest results. This led to an investigation by the engineering team, who discovered that the NPS survey was embedded in an iframe that had *cropped off the highest NPS response values*—so that it was physically (or, should we say, digitally?) impossible for a customer to choose 9 or 10.

- A ride-sharing company had built an ML model to detect potentially fraudulent new rider accounts and automatically block them from signing up. Their model relied on third-party credit card data. Among other things, the model learned that when the data from the third party was NULL, the likelihood of fraud was higher; it was a sign that the person was signing up with a card that might not be legitimate.

  Everything was working well until one day the third party had a data quality issue that caused it to send NULL data much more often than it had before. No one noticed the error, and the company continued using the ML model to make fraud predictions. This led to many new users being denied their ability to sign up for the company's services, as they were incorrectly classified as fraudulent accounts.

We bet every reader who works with data has had similar experiences. When data's done right, it unlocks incredible value. But when you have no quality assurance about your data, it's like trying to run a restaurant with ingredients that may or may not be contaminated. You might get lucky and no one will get sick—but some of the time, your customers and your business are liable to suffer, and you can bet they won't look at your food the same way again. One study found that 91% of IT decision makers (*https://oreil.ly/60PWo*) think they need to improve data quality at their company; 77% said they lack trust in their organization's business data.

Is there a way to bring back trust in data? And can you ensure that the kinds of issues we've just mentioned are detected immediately and resolved quickly, before anyone else is impacted, even (and especially) when you work with large volumes of complex data?

We believe the answer is yes, and the solution is to *automate your data quality monitoring with machine learning.* This book will help you discover the power of automated data quality monitoring. You'll learn how to implement a platform that will help ensure high-quality, trustworthy data for your business.

High-Quality Data Is the New Gold

It feels like only yesterday that businesses were struggling to get data out of isolated databases. Apache Hadoop made it possible to run more advanced queries on large and complex datasets (if you knew what you were doing). Despite this, in the recent past, data was generally limited to a small set of transactional systems—a "walled garden" of critical resources, tightly controlled, with limited access.

In a matter of years, cloud data warehouses/lakehouses and data transformation tools rapidly transformed how we work with data. Now, every scrap of information an organization touches is logged and stored. Any decision maker in the organization can either (a) pull up an interactive dashboard or report to answer questions with data or (b) directly query the data themselves. Machine learning systems, built on data, are informing or automating business decisions and powering new products.

"We firmly believe the next 10 years will be the decade of data," wrote Silicon Valley investment firm Andreessen Horowitz in 2022 (*https://oreil.ly/u4mX3*). The media loves to call data both the new oil and the new gold. We think there should be a major caveat on these kinds of statements: they're only right *if the data itself is high quality.* Bad data is worse than no data at all.

To see why, let's examine some of the trends happening around data and why quality is the make-or-break factor in each case.

Data-Driven Companies Are Today's Disrupters

The common storyline is that the fastest-growing, most successful companies today are software companies. But on closer examination, they're really *data* companies.

Consider Amazon. They didn't just build the world's largest retail platform by having world-class software engineering talent. They did it by figuring out how to harness data for personalized recommendations, real-time pricing, and optimized logistics. To pick an example from another industry, Capital One is one of the first US banks to move its data from on-premises systems to the cloud. They've been able to differentiate and accelerate their growth by using data to personalize marketing and make smarter underwriting decisions.

Whether you look at financial services, commerce, digital media, or healthcare, the intersection of data and software is the competitive frontier. However, businesses can't make good decisions, much less revolutionize an industry, if they're working with low-quality data that their own employees struggle to trust. It would be a mistake to invest in new data science, machine learning, and generative AI projects when your data quality foundation is rotten.

Data Analytics Is Democratized

Eager to keep up with the disrupters—or to become one—companies are asking every team to become more data driven. They've embedded analytics experts into functional units (marketing, growth, finance, product teams, etc.) to drive more sophisticated uses of data for decision making: Can we pull the stats on our customers' past browsing and purchase activity so that we write more tailored emails? Can we look at how our power users are adopting the latest feature to see if our launch was successful?

There are now a plethora of tools that let analysts—or truly anyone on a cross-functional team—self-serve the answers to data-related questions without writing any code. In seconds, they can spin up a dashboard or report that would have taken an engineer a month to build not so long ago. To support these analytics needs, data is no longer maintained by a small, centralized team or available as a consolidated fact table for the entire business. Instead, data is dispersed and managed by a wider group of people that sit closer to the business lines.

Without high-quality data, what we've seen is that democratization becomes a nightmare for data engineering teams. They're overwhelmed with a backlog of questions and always on edge for the next fire drill. Meanwhile, the rest of the organization grows more and more suspicious of the data the more they try to work with it. Heuristics and hunches become the norm once again. Ultimately, if there isn't trust in the data, democratizing analytics is a waste of time.

AI and Machine Learning Are Differentiators

Many companies have AI/ML on their road map because it can create incredible value in the form of personalized and automated interactions. Machine learning (or ML, which we will use interchangeably with AI) relies on advanced statistical models to predict the future based on historical signals in the data called *features*. With enough feature data and the right modeling techniques, AI can optimize or personalize any frequent interaction with an entity the business cares about (consumers, content, transactions, etc.).

Data quality makes or breaks ML models. You must ensure you have high-quality datasets for both training and inference. Models are quite good at performing well if the data they see in production matches the distribution of data they were trained upon. But models will tend to fail miserably when presented with data that is far outside of the distribution they have seen before. (Contrast this to humans, who can use higher-order intelligence to generalize from one domain or distribution to another and account for significant departures from the norm.)

Generative AI and data quality

Speaking of differentiators: What about generative AI? These models don't work like traditional ML. Rather than making predictions based on features that are engineered from structured data, they ingest raw, unstructured data directly—it's like drinking from the fire hose.

Is data quality still relevant if businesses are increasingly reliant on generative AI? The answer is a definitive yes. Prompts will need to incorporate structured data from the business (such as customer information). If you automate parts of your business with these models, you need ways to track that automation and ensure that things are working as expected through high-quality logs. And ultimately, even if generative AI lives up to or surpasses the hype, we're always going to need to be able to trust the data we aggregate, count, and analyze—like time and money.

Furthermore, there will still be data quality issues in the unstructured data organizations feed to these generative AI models. These will be even harder to find with traditional data quality monitoring approaches and will require automated ML or AI to identify them. This makes the techniques covered in this book all the more relevant as a foundation for ensuring that new generative AI applications are working with high-quality inputs.

Companies Are Investing in a Modern Data Stack

No summary of data trends today would be complete without a mention of the modern data stack (even though we can't wait for this term to go out of style, to be completely honest!). Today, the right set of software as a service (SaaS) vendors can accomplish what a 100-person team of full-time data engineers would have done 10 years ago. Businesses are migrating from legacy on-prem storage to cloud systems that let them leverage more data more easily than ever before.

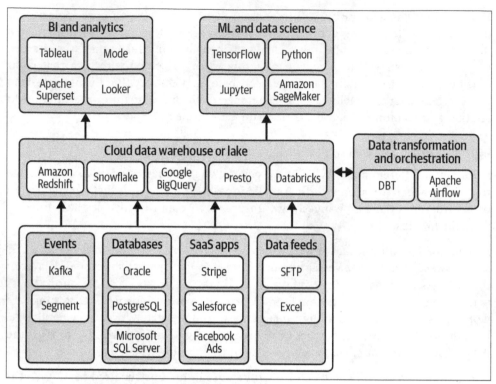

Figure 1-1. The modern data stack.

The modern data stack is a major investment. This investment is undermined when tools for data quality are left out of the picture (as in Figure 1-1). Especially because migrations can be a major source of data quality issues, organizations often end up with data that's in a bad state post-upgrade (see the section "Data Migrations" on page 9). Tracing the root cause of problems is even harder in a brand-new system where everyone is learning the ropes.

Broken machines
> Data processing or orchestration tools can break down entirely, stopping or degrading the flow of data.

Scheduling errors
> Data processing jobs can run out of order or with the wrong cadence, causing missing data, incorrect computations, or duplicate data.

Poor raw materials
> Raw data fed into the factory can be of poor quality due to upstream issues, and the adverse effects can propagate throughout the rest of the warehouse.

Incorrect parts
> Errors can be introduced into the SQL, Spark, or other code that is processing and manipulating the data, causing invalid joins, transformations, or aggregations.

Incorrect settings
> Engineers can make mistakes in the configuration of complex data processing jobs, which can lead to a wide variety of issues.

Botched upgrades
> Attempts to upgrade code, application versions, or entire subsystems can introduce subtle but pervasive differences in how data is encoded or transformed.

Communication failures
> Well-intentioned changes to add new features or functionality can be communicated poorly to other affected teams, leading to inconsistencies in data processing logic that create quality issues.

Issues inside the data factory are often the most common sources of data quality incidents, as they directly affect the flow and contents of the data (and can be very difficult to test outside of a production data environment).

Data Migrations

Data migrations are occurring more frequently as companies seek to keep up with the latest and greatest infrastructure. This includes moving from an on-premises data warehouse to a cloud provider (e.g., Teradata to Snowflake), from one cloud provider to another (e.g., Amazon Web Services [AWS] to Google Cloud Platform [GCP] or vice versa), from one database to another (e.g., PostgreSQL to AWS Aurora), or from one database version to another (e.g., Elasticsearch cluster migrations).

All of these migrations are prone to data quality issues. Let's take a look at migrating from on-premises data warehouses to cloud/SaaS providers. Many companies have very complex data pipelines originating from mainframe legacy systems that were transferred into increasingly legacy on-prem data warehouses. These legacy systems have been in place for decades and have accumulated a tremendous amount of incremental complexity as new features have been added, teams have come and gone, and business requirements have changed.

When moving this tangled web of data processing and storage into the cloud, companies seek to replicate what was done in their on-prem environment. But there can be very subtle issues introduced in re-creating the on-prem flows in the cloud, leading to major data quality consequences.

For example, one company we work with mentioned that their customers' dates of birth were mangled badly by such a migration (visualized in Figure 1-3). In their legacy mainframe, birthdates were stored as integers offset from a certain reference date, such as January 1, 1900. Upon export, those integers were then converted into dates in the new cloud warehouse. This seemed easy enough, except that unbeknownst to anyone, the cloud data warehouse automatically used the Unix timestamp reference of 1970 as the offset. All the birthdates were pushed far into the future.

As with many data quality issues, the repercussions happened later, and silently. The company had a marketing application that would send emails to customers based on their age. Once this app was pointed to the new cloud data warehouse, *no* customers received *any* emails until someone noticed the problem. (Marketing teams often end up bearing a significant amount of pain from poor data quality. One survey found (*https://oreil.ly/idW6e*) that marketers were wasting 21% of their total budget on data issues.)

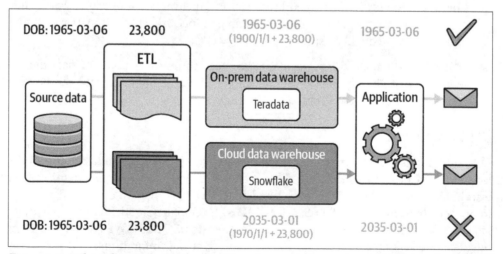

Figure 1-3. When data stored in an on-prem data warehouse is migrated to a cloud data warehouse, discrepancies can arise, such as in this example involving different reference dates for calculating customers' birthdates.

Third-Party Data Sources

Using third-party data—that is, data that comes from outside the company—is easier and more common than ever. To give some examples, while Jeremy was at Instacart, third-party data regularly collected included:

- Weather data for demand forecasting/scheduling
- Third-party services for maps information for routing
- Consumer packaged goods (CPG) product catalog data for enriching the user search and shopping experience
- Fraud propensity scoring data for avoiding charge-backs
- Retailer inventory data for determining what's on the shelf at each store location at a given time

Frequently, third-party data is codified as a data relationship between two partners: company A and company B have to work together to service customer X or achieve operation Y, and that requires exchanging data. Sometimes, this is called *second-party data.*

In other cases, you are consuming public data or data packaged by a third-party service provider to be resold in a one-to-many relationship, often to make decisions about entities (customers, companies, locations) about which you have limited information. If you browse the publicly available feeds on the online catalog Demyst (*https://oreil.ly/2g4vc*), you'll see that it's possible to leverage comprehensive tax, property, and business data all with just a few clicks.

Third-party data is a common source of data quality problems. That's not only because providers make mistakes, but also because they often make changes, for example, to their APIs or data formats. Unless you have a very clear data contract in place, third parties won't necessarily be thinking about how their updates might affect your specific use case, nor will they be beholden to provide notice or mitigations.

Company Growth and Change

We'd argue that *almost all data begins as high quality*. When a product is first built and instrumented, the data captured about that product by the engineer who built it is usually very closely aligned with their intention and the product's function.

But data does not exist in a vacuum. In the real world, a company is constantly adapting and improving its products, which in turn affects the data emitted by those products. It's like the second law of thermodynamics: the entropy of the data will always increase over time. As time passes, the following factors cause the data quality to degrade:

New features

New features often expand the scope of the data the system is capturing. Insofar as this is an "add additional columns" type of change, the data quality risk isn't high. However, in some cases, new features may replace existing functionality, which tends to have a sudden impact on the data emitted by the system. In many cases, the new features may change the shape of the data. The granularity level might increase—such as data now being captured at the level of an item rather than the level of the entire product. Or what was previously a single message may be broken apart and restructured into many messages.

Bug fixes

The average piece of commercial software contains 20–30 bugs for every 1,000 lines of code (*https://oreil.ly/YeuIZ*), according to Carnegie Mellon University's CyLab Sustainable Computing Consortium. Bug fixes can have the same impact as new features. They can also genuinely improve data quality—but when that sudden improvement comes as a "shock" to the systems that depend on the data, there may be negative consequences (see the section "Data Shocks" on page 16).

Refactors

Refactoring happens when teams want to improve the structure of the code or systems behind an application without changing the functionality. However, refactors often present the risk of unintended changes—especially to things like data capture that may not be robustly tested in the application code.

Optimizations

Frequently, changes are made simply to improve the speed or efficiency of an application. In many cases, how data is being captured can be a performance issue, and changes can affect the reliability, temporal granularity, or uniqueness of the data emitted by the system.

New teams

New teams often inherit a legacy application and arrive with a limited understanding of how it interacts with other systems or how the data it produces is consumed. They may unintentionally break with existing expectations from other teams as they make changes to their product, introducing data quality issues.

Outages

In addition to intentional changes, many systems will simply have outages where they stop functioning or function in a degraded level of service. Data capture is often lost entirely during these outages. This is often not a data quality issue per se, as the lack of data is a reflection of the lack of activity due to the outage. But in many cases, the outage may affect the data being emitted without affecting the service itself, which *is* a data quality issue.

A Tangled Web of Data

When it comes to data, it's unhelpful to think about a single system in isolation. Each product is part of a web of many systems that interact with each other by passing data back and forth (in real time or by batching up requests). Therefore, what a system emits as data is a function not only of its behavior but also of *how it interacts with all the other systems in the network it is connected to.*

Engineers and product managers making a change typically understand the implications of that change on their own systems. But what about the implications that spread throughout the application or organization? Teams' abilities to understand and foresee these implications will decrease as we move further away from their area of ownership.

For example, if the product catalog team at an ecommerce company makes a change to how their data is structured, they might understand how this would affect the company's product recommendation systems, which they work with frequently. But how likely are they to have insight into the implications for the advertising team selling targeted ads? What about the consequences for the fulfillment team that's optimizing how orders are routed—and is part of a completely different division?

At a large company, anticipating all the implications of a data change is nearly impossible. Most teams make a best effort and move on. Thus, as organizations get bigger, their data quality problems grow.

Exogenous Factors

When you leverage data to make decisions or build products, there will always be factors that affect the data that are outside of your control, such as user behavior, global events, competitor actions, and supplier and market forces. Note that these aren't data quality issues per se, but they often look and feel like data quality issues and may need to be handled in a similar way.

For example, in some industries, companies make automated decisions based on real-time data about what competitors are doing. Ecommerce companies monitor competitor price data and, in response, adjust their prices almost instantaneously. Airlines do the same. In these scenarios, if a competitor changes their behavior in a sudden, drastic manner, the business will immediately do the same—and end up with a large shift in their data. It's important for companies to be notified about these changes, as they may not always be desirable or intended.

Any discussion about exogenous factors would be remiss not to mention the COVID-19 pandemic. Everyone had to treat the beginning months of COVID-19 as a special case when analyzing user behavior. For example, Figure 1-4 shows how data about the number of miles logged for Chicago taxi trips changed dramatically in March 2020.

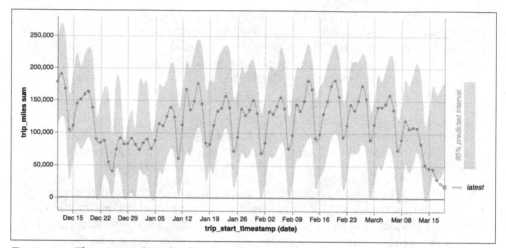

Figure 1-4. The average length of a taxi trip in Chicago plummeted in March 2020. The taxi data is publicly available from the city of Chicago website (https://oreil.ly/mQDTq). See a full-sized version of this image at https://oreil.ly/adqm_1_4.

During COVID-19, machine learning models had to be quickly retrained on fresh data, since their assumptions based on historical trends no longer applied. In one well-known case, Zillow's model for predicting housing prices—which was powering a new business arm, Zillow Offers—couldn't adapt fast enough. The automated service overpaid for homes that it didn't end up being able to sell in the changing market, and sadly Zillow had to lay off almost a quarter of its workforce as a result (*https://oreil.ly/oncgk*).

Teams typically find themselves in one of two situations regarding external factors:

- In some cases, like with COVID-19, external changes are dramatic enough that you need to put your decision-making processes on notice and possibly retrain your ML models. It's almost like a data quality issue—it's a change that you want to be immediately notified about so that you can do damage control.

- In other cases, external factors have a more subtle influence, such as a supply-chain issue affecting your order processing times. You need to quickly understand the context of these changes and rule out any data quality problems, which can often look like real external trends.

Why We Need Data Quality Monitoring

With the ever-increasing importance of high-quality data, and the fact that data quality problems are more prolific than ever, you might already be convinced that improving data quality is important. But how should you think about such an initiative? Is it as a one-time fix—getting your data into shape over a period of months or quarters, and letting things run smoothly from there?

This kind of approach often makes sense for software, but much less so for data. Code is the same today as it is tomorrow, barring a deliberate update. You can test it in a controlled QA environment and also run unit tests that isolate just one part of the system. Once your tests pass, you're essentially done.

Data, on the other hand, is chaotic and constantly changing. It's dependent on external factors you don't control, such as how users interact with your product in real time, so you can really only test it holistically in production. Your tests have to be able to filter out all the noise—and there's a lot of noise—from the true data quality signal.

For this reason, while software bugs are often quickly detected and fixed through automated testing and user feedback, *we strongly believe that the vast majority of data quality issues are never caught.* Because teams lack the right continuous monitoring tools for data, problems happen silently and go unnoticed.

Making matters worse, the cost of fixing a data quality issue increases dramatically the more time has passed since the issue occurred:

- The number of potential changes that could have caused the issue goes up linearly with the length of time over which you are evaluating.
- The amount of context the team has on why a change was made, or what the implications of that change could be, goes down with the time since the change.
- The cost to "fix" the issue (including backfilling the data) goes up with the amount of time since the issue was first introduced.
- Issues that persist for long periods of time end up becoming "normal behavior" to other downstream systems, so fixing them may cause new incidents.

When an incident is introduced and then fixed later, it really has two different types of impact. We call these data scars and data shocks.

Data Scars

After an incident happens, unless the data is painstakingly repaired (which is often impossible or expensive to do), it will leave a *scar* in the data. We first heard this term used by Daniele Perito, chief data officer and cofounder of Faire. A scar is a period of time for a given set of data where a subset of records are invalid or anomalous and cannot be trusted by any systems operating on those records in the future.

Data scars will impact ML models, as those models will have to adapt to learn different relationships in the data during the period of the scar. This will weaken their performance and limit their ability to learn from all the data captured during the scar. It will also dampen the model's belief in the importance of the features affected by the scar—the model will underweight these inputs, wrongly believing they're less prevalent in the dataset. Even if you manage to go back in time and repair the scar, it's easy to introduce what's known as *data leakage* into downstream ML applications by inadvertently including some current state information in your fix. This leads to the model performing very well in offline evaluations (since it has access to "time-traveled" information from the future) but acting erratically in production (where it no longer has this information).

Data scars will also greatly impact any future analytics or data science work done on this dataset. They may lead to more complex data pipelines that are harder to write and maintain, as data users have to add a lot of exception handling to avoid biases introduced by the scar. These exceptions may need to be noted and addressed in any reporting or visualizations that include data from the time of the scar, increasing cognitive overhead on anyone trying to interpret the data or make decisions from it. Or, scars may need to be removed entirely from the dataset, leading to "data amnesia" from that period, which can affect trend analysis or time-based comparisons (e.g., what was our year-over-year result for this statistic?).

Data Shocks

In addition to the scarring effect, there are also effects in production that occur both when the data quality issue was introduced *and* when the data issue is fixed. This is what we call a data quality *shock*, and it can also affect AI/ML and decision making.

When the data quality issue first occurs, any ML models that use features derived from the data will suddenly be presented with data that is entirely different from what they were trained on. This will cause them to be "shocked" by the new data, and they will produce predictions that are often wildly inaccurate for any observations affected by the data quality incident. This shock will last until the models are retrained using new data, which often happens automatically in a continuous deployment model.

Then, once the data quality is fixed, that actually introduces yet another shock to the model (unless the data is repaired historically, which often isn't possible). The shock from the fix can often be as bad as the initial shock from the introduction of the data quality issue!

For analytics/reporting use cases, these shocks often manifest as metrics or analyses that have sudden unexpected changes. When these are observed, they are often mistaken for real-world changes (the whole purpose of these reports is to reflect what's happening in reality), so operations are changed or other decisions are made to respond to the data quality issue as though it were real. Again, the same thing can happen in reverse when the fix is released.

The longer the data quality issue goes unfixed, the deeper the scar, and the greater the shock from fixing it.

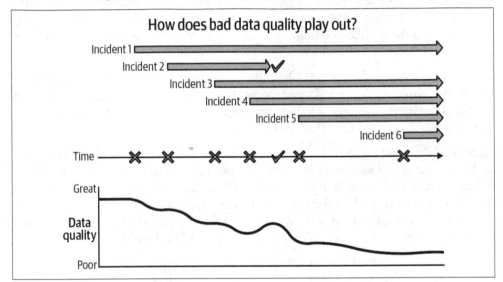

Figure 1-5. How incidents accumulate to erode data quality and trust over time. Each bar is a data scar left by the incident. Each X (marking when the incident first occurred) is a data shock. Notably, the checkmark (when Incident 2 was resolved) is also a data shock.

The implication of allowing scars and shocks to continue accumulating is that slowly, over time, the objective quality of the data erodes. Figure 1-5 illustrates how incidents pile up such that everyone becomes convinced that the data quality is low and the data itself is untrustworthy. And as hard as it is to backfill data, it's even harder to backfill trust.

Therefore, there's a framing change needed in how organizations think about combating poor data quality. It shouldn't be a one-off project to go in and fix data quality for a given data source. It needs to instead be a continuous data quality monitoring initiative, where data quality issues are found as they occur and resolved as quickly as possible.

Without data quality monitoring, issues will go uncaught until a business user, data professional, or customer of the ML algorithm or other systems notices. Operating a data factory in this way is akin to running a factory making a consumer good without any quality control processes.

Automating Data Quality Monitoring: The New Frontier

Data professionals today are experiencing exciting, downright astonishing changes in the field. Whether it's investing in generative AI, democratizing analytics across the business, or migrating from a legacy database to the cloud, almost every company out there is in the middle of doing something new with data that they've never done before.

For most enterprises, therefore, the best time to invest in data quality is now. As your use of data grows, so do the risks and the negative impact of data quality issues. Data quality is something that needs to be monitored constantly and maintained diligently by fixing problems as soon as they arise.

Effective data quality monitoring is no easy task—especially at the scale of thousands of tables and billions of records, which is common for a large enterprise. While it might be obvious that it doesn't work to have humans manually inspect your data, it also doesn't work to use legacy solutions like writing tests for your data and tracking key metrics. You may want to do this for your most important tables, but implementing it for your entire data warehouse simply isn't feasible.

In this book, we'll introduce you to the concept of automating data quality monitoring with unsupervised ML. This is a new technique with many benefits. It requires hardly any manual setup and scales easily across your data warehouse. With the right implementation, it automatically learns the appropriate thresholds for whether a data change is big enough to signal a quality issue. It can detect a broad range of problems, including *unknown unknowns* that no one has ever thought to write a test for.

Using ML comes with its own challenges. Building the model is a complicated task on its own, but you'll also need to ensure it works on a wide variety of real-world data without over- or under-alerting. You'll want to build out notifications that help your team effectively triage issues, and integrations with your data toolkit that bring data quality front and center for your organization. And you'll need to have a plan in place to deploy and manage your monitoring platform in the long term.

Don't worry—we're here to help with the advice and tools you'll need along the way. We think automating data quality monitoring with ML is just as exciting as any data innovation that has happened in the past several years and one of the most important breakthroughs in the modern data stack. By the end of this book, we hope you'll agree.

## CHAPTER 2

Data Quality Monitoring Strategies and the Role of Automation

There are many different ways you can approach data quality monitoring. Before evaluating the options, it helps to think about what success looks like. In this chapter, we'll define the requirements for success. Then we'll walk through the traditional strategies—manual checks, rule-based testing, and metrics monitoring—and see how they measure up.

Next, we'll explore the idea of *automating* data quality monitoring. We'll explain how unsupervised machine learning can help us satisfy some missing aspects of our success criteria, scaling monitoring to large amounts of data while reducing alert fatigue.

We'll wrap up by introducing the data quality monitoring strategy we advocate for in this book: a four-pillar approach combining data observability, rule-based testing, metrics monitoring, and unsupervised machine learning. As we'll show, this approach has many advantages. It allows subject matter experts (SMEs) to enforce essential constraints and track key performance indicators (KPIs) for important tables—all while providing a base level of monitoring for a large volume of diverse data. No server farms or legions of analysts required.

Monitoring Requirements

To address the vast array of problems outlined in Chapter 1, a successful data quality monitoring strategy must deliver across four dimensions (as shown in Figure 2-1):

- First, it must *detect* quality issues in all your important data so that you can be confident no issues are slipping through the cracks—whether they appear at the level of tables, columns, or individual rows.

- Second, it must *alert* the right people in a timely manner when there is a real issue, without causing *alert fatigue* by notifying people about nonissues.
- Third, it must help you *resolve* issues quickly and efficiently. (For a complete list of what these issues could be, see the Appendix.)
- And finally, it must *scale* to monitor the health of your data enterprise-wide.

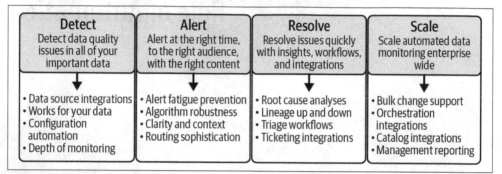

Figure 2-1. A data quality monitoring solution should succeed across the four dimensions of detect, alert, resolve, and scale.

Alert Fatigue

When a data quality monitoring solution fails to alert on a real issue, it's called a false negative. When a solution triggers an alert when it shouldn't have—for an issue that users don't care about or that isn't really a problem at all—this is called a false positive (see Figure 2-2 for a visual).

A system with many false positives is arguably just as problematic as a system with many false negatives because it will bombard users with unhelpful alerts, leading to the undesirable condition of *alert fatigue*. This is when users become so tired of responding to false alarms that they begin to ignore notifications from the system or, worse, disable notifications entirely. It's a bit like the platform that cried wolf. Data quality monitoring systems are particularly susceptible to alert fatigue, and it's one of the most common reasons that adoption of a monitoring system fails.

For more on reducing alert fatigue and ensuring notifications are high value, see Chapter 6.

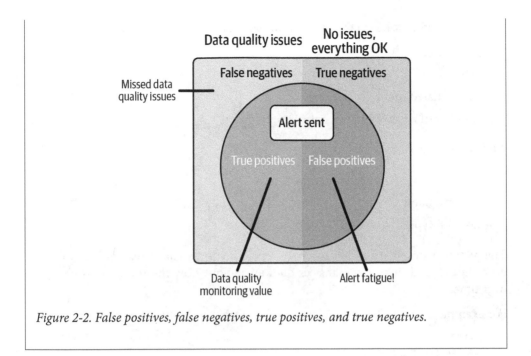

Figure 2-2. False positives, false negatives, true positives, and true negatives.

Data Observability: Necessary, but Not Sufficient

Before talking about data quality monitoring approaches, let's touch on data observability. It's a key part of any comprehensive data quality strategy, with the important distinction that data observability *monitors metadata about your tables, not the contents of the data itself.*

Data observability is similar to infrastructure or networking observability but applied to data in a data warehouse. Namely, it's about answering the following questions:

- Does this table still exist?
- Have there been any adverse changes to the schema of the table?
- Has the table been updated recently?
- Is the volume of data in the table consistent with my expectations?

These are important questions when determining whether you can trust your data, and you'll notice that some of the data issues in the Appendix can be detected with observability alone.

So, how does data observability work? Fortunately, the metadata it uses can be gathered from most modern data warehouses *without having to query the table at all.* There's typically either an API that makes this data available or a system view that can be queried that keeps this data up to date. The data needed includes table-level statistics like:

- Table
- Last updated time
- Number of rows (or size in bytes)

And column-level information like:

- Table
- Column name
- Column type

The platform simply needs to capture observability metadata at regular intervals (say, every hour), and then it can answer questions about how the metadata is changing over time.

For example, in Snowflake, you can retrieve the table-level metadata using this query:

```
SELECT
    TABLE_NAME,
    ROW_COUNT,
    BYTES,
    LAST_ALTERED
FROM INFORMATION_SCHEMA."TABLES"
```

When it comes to "Has the table been updated recently?," the system needs to make a tough decision: What does "recently" mean, and when has a delay become significant? Some tables are updated continuously using streaming data. Others are updated every hour. Others may be updated multiple times per day, or only multiple times per week (or month, or year). Time series models (as discussed in the sidebar "Time Series Metric Monitoring" on page 31) are a powerful tool here—they can use the history of updates to predict the expected upper bound for when the next update will arrive.

Something similar has to be done to decide if the volume of data "is consistent with expectations." A time series model can observe the volume history and identify if the most recent update is anomalously low. Once these problems have been addressed, data observability can be applied to thousands, or even tens of thousands, of tables in a data warehouse.

Does this mean you've solved data quality? Of course not! Data observability checks are just about the flow of data through your warehouse. They don't address whether the contents of that data are high quality. Using only data observability would be akin to operating a water treatment plant where your only quality control was the water pressure you delivered—with no concern about whether that water was even potable!

Table 2-1 reiterates the key differences between data observability and data quality monitoring.

Table 2-1. The differences between data observability and data quality monitoring

	Data observability	Data quality monitoring
What it answers	Is data moving through my warehouse in a timely manner?	Is the data my warehouse produces of high quality?
How it works	Catalog metadata Job monitoring Data lineage	Queries the data Requires experts or ML Explainability is key
Why it's needed	Catches data *movement* failures	Does deep monitoring of data values
Major drawback	Ignores data *contents*	Difficult to scale

Traditional Approaches to Data Quality

Many teams find it relatively easy to implement data observability for their entire warehouse but struggle when it comes to scaling their data quality monitoring. Historically, the most common ways that teams have approached data quality monitoring are through manual detection, rule-based testing, and metrics monitoring. While we present these strategies separately here, organizations often employ a mix of all three at once. There is value in each of these strategies, but also significant drawbacks at scale.

Manual Data Quality Detection

Since the invention of digital data, it's been possible—but increasingly difficult—for humans to comb through data by hand and find potential issues.

At some businesses, there's an intentional process of manual data quality review, whether in the form of spot-checking, reviewing summaries, or looking at visualizations. This generally isn't sufficient for monitoring data quality. Manual inspection might work when the data is small and simple enough that a human can look at a spreadsheet and quickly spot potential issues (by the way, various studies report (*https://oreil.ly/oEMGS*) that nearly 90% of spreadsheets contain errors!). But it's not effective at scale. Furthermore, a manual process is inherently subjective. Give the same complex dataset to 10 different analysts, and you'll get a large number of divergent conclusions about the quality of the data they are evaluating.

Manual data quality detection also happens in a very different way: by accident. Someone is in the midst of doing something with the data, and they "stumble upon" a data quality issue. Here are a few examples:

Computing summary statistics and comparing these to known figures or other reference data points

For instance, a data scientist might find that the number of customers is 50% higher in an aggregated dataset than in another known source, indicating there must be a data quality issue.

Creating visualizations that summarize the data in ways that make it clear that there are data quality issues

For example, a visualization of missing values over time may show a very sharp increase in recent weeks.

Reaching conclusions from an analysis, or from interrogating models, that suggest things that are provably untrue

An analyst might find that growth in new accounts exceeded 1,000% per week in Europe for the last three weeks, and yet there is no possible way that could happen. Or an ML model might suggest that the most important feature in predicting user churn is a user's date of birth—but on closer inspection, this is due to a large fraction of users being born on January 1, 1970 (the beginning of the Unix epoch, indicating bad data).

Relying on analysts and data scientists to discover data quality issues as they work is not a winning strategy either. Practitioners will examine the data only periodically, and with a very specific purpose in mind. They will most likely catch data quality issues long after they've occurred and will almost certainly miss data quality issues that are outside the scope of their project.

This kind of resolve-as-you-go approach is actually quite detrimental. In some organizations we've worked with, *more than 50%* of analysts' time is dedicated to investigating and working around data quality issues. Not only does this manual work cut the team's effectiveness in half, but over time it takes a huge toll on morale.

All this being said, analysts and data scientists invariably want visibility into the data they work with, and depending on the situation, a manual review can add value. Humans are capable of bringing together disparate data sources and contextual knowledge and drawing conclusions in ways that algorithms are unable to automate. Plus, when data quality issues are found in the context of an analysis or ML model, they are by definition "important" data quality issues that need to be addressed—there's no risk of false positives.

Ultimately, whatever monitoring approach you choose should reduce manual effort and make it possible to monitor data at scale. However, it should still make it easy for humans to profile their data and spot issues manually, and you can aid this process by producing summary statistics and visualizations.

Rule-Based Testing

When testing software, engineers write unit tests that invoke components, measure the actions taken, and apply deterministic rules to those measurements to validate that the software is working as expected. For example, an ecommerce application might have a method for computing the tax rate. A unit test could supply this method with various baskets of goods and store locations and ensure that it produces the right answer.

It's natural to try to take what works for testing software—writing lots of unit tests— and apply that to data. We call this approach *rule-based testing*. Common tools for rule-based testing include Great Expectations and dbt. A rule-based test is a deterministic test that can be applied to data from a specific source. The data either passes the test or fails the test; there is no gray area in between.

Examples of rule-based tests include:

- The column `number_of_tickets` in the table `ticket_sales` is never NULL.
- There are no values in the column `listing_time` that are from the future.
- The average of the column `price_per_ticket` is always between 50 and 100 every day.
- The result of the equation `number_of_tickets * price_per_ticket * (1 + tax_rate)` is always equal to `total_price` for every row in the table `ticket_sales`.

Every rule can be thought of as having a scope, a type, and (usually) a number of constraints:

Scope
What data does the rule apply to? What data store? What table or view? What column(s)? For what time range? For which specific rows?

Note that in most cases, rule-based tests can be evaluated for each row of a given dataset, which allows you to cleanly separate "good" rows from "bad" rows. But rules can also be applied to statistics computed from the data (e.g., `0 <= sum(col umn_x) <= 50`). In general, we'll talk about rules as applying to each row of the data independently. The special case of applying a rule to a statistic can be viewed as first computing an aggregated dataset (which could be aggregated by some entity, like a customer; or a unit of time, like a date; or without any grouping at all) and then applying a row-based rule to the result of that aggregate.

Type
What is the type of rule that will be applied? For example, for rules that apply to a given column, you could choose from a variety of types: column is unique,

column never contains NULL values, column string values are within a specified set, etc. Rule types can extend beyond individual columns, covering metadata about the table (last updated time, total number of rows), the schema of the table (specific column names, types, and order), and much more. Rules can involve multiple columns and their relations to one another, or how the table relates to other tables via join semantics (e.g., joins 1:1 on a given primary key).

The most complex types of rules are often expressed as SQL queries that may include joins, subqueries, and complex statements that look for conditions that should "never appear" in the table. For example: "Every customer that has an order that completed checkout and was not subsequently canceled, voided, or completed should have a record in the customers_with_active_orders table."

This can be represented in SQL as:

```
SELECT COUNT(DISTINCT customer_id) as num_missing
FROM orders
WHERE checked_out
AND order_status NOT IN ('canceled', 'voided', 'completed')
AND customer_id NOT IN
    (SELECT customer_id FROM customers_with_active_orders)
```

Constraint

Once you've chosen the scope and type, you often have to provide some constant constraints to the rule. For example, in the rule "price_per_ticket is always between 50 and 100," the values of 50 and 100 are the constant constraints. In some cases, these aren't necessary ("column X is unique" doesn't require a constraint) or they are redundant with the rule type ("column is never NULL" is equivalent to "NULL count is equal to 0," where 0 is the constant).

Rules are an essential part of any data quality monitoring strategy. Compared to human analysis, rules are cheap to run and don't make mistakes. Rules are also clear and deterministic. Each row either passes or doesn't. Once you fully grok the rule, you also understand why the rule-based test would fail, and what would need to be true in order for the test to pass for that row. When a rule-based test fails, you can trust that it truly failed—it's impossible for there to be a false positive where the data was good but the rule said it was bad (unless, of course, the rule itself is incorrect; we'll address that shortly).

Additionally, rules are one of the most reliable ways to identify historical data quality issues that have existed from the beginning of a dataset or were never caught and addressed historically. Why? Rules allow an SME to express a requirement that they have for a given dataset, based on their knowledge of the system that generated the data or the business context in which the data was collected. An SME can write a rule saying that a column should never be NULL in the data's past, present, or future. Contrast this with approaches that learn from the history of the data (such as using metrics or unsupervised ML to detect unexpected changes, both of which we'll address in a moment). Those approaches are inherently looking for sudden changes in the data, which are by definition *new* rather than historical data quality issues. Such approaches cannot tell if the data was always bad.

Rules are also good at identifying the needle in the haystack. If you're working with a table that has billions of rows, then a rule is often the most reliable way to spot if there are a handful of records that violate a given condition. (Note that this can be a liability if you don't care about each and every record, as you'll have to find ways to exclude data quality "scars" from the past that you no longer care about but that violate your rule.)

Relying solely on rule-based testing, however, is a mistake. For one thing, there's a lot of room for error in specifying high-quality rules:

- The *scope* can be too narrowly specified (too tight a WHERE SQL clause), causing the rule to miss data quality issues (e.g., the rule was only applied to segment X of a table, but it should also apply to segment Y).

- The *scope* can be too widely specified (too expansive a WHERE SQL clause), causing the rule to incorrectly flag valid data as invalid (e.g., this column actually *should* be NULL for certain records).

- The *constraint* of the rule can be incorrectly specified. This is very common when setting ranges for column values or for statistics. The range may be too wide (and thus miss real data quality issues), or too narrow (and thus be very noisy as data changes).

- The wrong *type* of rule may be selected. The test may either fail to capture the real intent of the user or produce notifications that are not meaningful because the test was inappropriate (the column was always intended to have NULL values, but a "never NULL" rule was applied anyway).

Furthermore, covering all of a modern enterprise's data with high-quality rules is a Sisyphean task. Consider the following realistic hypothetical example, where an organization has 10,000 tables to monitor for data quality issues:

- 10 tables are mission-critical fact tables that the entire company depends on (key statistics aggregated for the board come from these tables).

- 90 tables contain critical data used to make business and operational decisions on a daily basis across the company.

- 900 tables are of critical importance to individual teams or initiatives, used by product managers, ML engineers, analysts, data scientists, or other data-savvy professionals on a weekly basis.

- The remaining 9,000 tables could have data quality issues that manifest in subtle, difficult-to-detect ways in the other 1,000 tables.

Each of these tables might have tens, hundreds, or even thousands of columns. For example, fact tables often aggregate a wide variety of information about a given type of entity into a single very broad table that launches many analyses and use cases. Some tables can also have hundreds or thousands of segments (groups of rows) that have different behavior. Web event tables, for instance, often capture a large volume of structured data (device, IP address, URL, user, time, etc.) and semistructured data (JSON payloads) for hundreds or thousands of different events or actions that users can take.

Each column or segment of data for each table might require 5 to 10 rules to cover the most important constraints on that data. Thus, to monitor their most important tables with rule-based testing, an organization could end up writing *1,000 tables * 50 columns per table * 5 rules per column = 250,000 rules*. And this doesn't cover semistructured data, segment variation, or the other 9,000 potentially important tables!

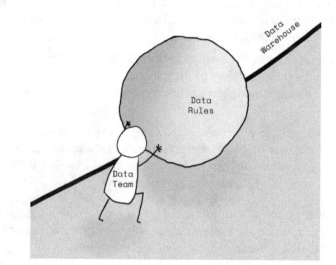

The Sisyphean task of creating and maintaining data quality rules in large warehouses (illustration by Josie Stanley)

In addition to creating rule-based tests, you have to maintain them, which is much more difficult than maintaining unit tests. A unit test for code should produce the same result every time it's run, until there's a software update that breaks the expected behavior, intentionally or unintentionally. But unlike code, data changes constantly and in unpredictable ways—as new products are launched, the macroenvironment shifts, or user behavior changes, to name a few reasons. Therefore, rule-based tests can be very brittle. To ensure that their definitions—and particularly their constraints—remain accurate, rules need to be constantly updated as the product and data evolve. It can be tempting to save some time by loosening the constraints up front, but this risks missing real issues.

In summary, rule-based testing is not a scalable solution to monitoring data in a modern enterprise. However, rules are a powerful tool for SMEs to express and enforce their expectations of the data from first principles. For example, Figure 2-3, from Airbnb's report of its data quality strategy, gives practical examples of SME-defined rules that enforce consistency in listings data. The ideal data quality solution makes it easy for rules to be created, edited, and analyzed by a diverse audience of SMEs.

Data Quality Checks

Automated data validation will include the following checks.

Pre-checks on source data

- Partition-level run-time checks for service data exports
- Time series anomaly detection for "active_listings" in listing service export

Stage-check-exchange paradigm for production dataset

- After data has landed in staging, we perform extensive partition-level run-time checks, and fail the pipeline if any test fails:
    - Standard list of run-time checks
    - Perfect consistency between all metrics [e.g. active(ds) = active(ds-1) + new_active_listings + reactivations - deactivations] (See equations in definitions)

Anomaly detection on staged data

- Time series analysis for each of the following metrics: number of active listings, new active listings, reactivations and deactivations, as well as row counts for all tables
- Warn if large deviation outside 99% confidence interval, fail if outside max threshold
- Once all staging checks have run, exchange data into production using the exchange operator

---

Figure 2-3. An excerpt from the Medium post "Data Quality at Airbnb" (https://oreil.ly/eTed_) that shows examples of validation rules and metrics checks that Airbnb runs to ensure data quality internally.

Metrics Monitoring

The next data quality monitoring approach is also inspired by software engineering. Most software systems are monitored by tracking metrics about the infrastructure and notifying when there are sudden adverse changes. These stats could be about the hardware itself (CPU utilization, memory, etc.), the networking activities (packets lost, etc.), or individual services that are running (queue length, average latency, etc.).

Analogously, you can monitor statistics about data and set thresholds to tell the system to alert if the data spikes above or below expectations. The challenge is that, for data quality, the surface area of metrics to monitor explodes. To ensure proper coverage, you need metrics for every column, segment, and statistic you might care about—such as percentage of NULL values, percentage of duplicates, mean, min/max, etc.

Beyond the scalability issues, metrics monitoring for data quality presents other problems, too. For one thing, because it tests the data at the aggregate statistical level, it may miss data quality issues that affect only a small percentage of the records. Furthermore, most implementations of metrics monitoring don't identify the specific records that were responsible for the metric changing—making it hard to understand why metrics changed and whether the reason was valid (such as an external trend) or due to a data quality issue.

Metrics monitoring can also miss issues that creep into the data over time. For example, imagine the source of a data quality issue is a code change that's behind a feature flag. If the feature is slowly rolled out to customer segments, the data will change gradually. Any change to the metrics will also be slow and might never reach the threshold for an alert.

That said, metrics monitoring is essential when you want to pay close attention to a very specific slice of the data. For example, Figure 3-1 shows some of the metrics that Airbnb has chosen to prioritize, such as number of active listings, new active listings, reactivations, and deactivations. Important metrics like these are often heavily influenced by a small subset of the overall dataset, and any trends therein might not be caught by other monitoring methods that consider the data as a whole.

Similarly, metrics monitoring can help when the data is degraded for some expected percentage of records, but the user wants to avoid that percentage going up in a significant way. For example, it could be that 20% of the time, user records don't have a valid address because of how those user records are created. If that percentage were to increase significantly, then there might be a data quality issue that has corrupted or removed address information for a larger number of users than expected.

Given these pros and cons, a successful data quality monitoring strategy should let users set up monitoring on key metrics and, ideally, use time series models to set appropriate thresholds. But it's not enough to rely on metrics monitoring alone.

Time Series Metric Monitoring

Configuring metrics thresholds by hand tends to be brittle, for the same reason that manual constraints on rules are hard to maintain: most datasets are highly seasonal and change rapidly. Rather than having the user set a hard-and-fast range that the statistic must fall into, many metrics monitoring strategies use a time series model.

Time series modeling, also called sequence modeling, evaluates a time series history of values and then predicts an expected range of values at some point in the future. There are a variety of methods for producing time series models:

- Traditional methods like exponential smoothing and autoregressive integrated moving average (ARIMA) (*https://oreil.ly/UTTXc*)
- Additive approaches that decompose a time series into components (e.g., Facebook's Prophet (*https://oreil.ly/UYbHY*))
- Black box approaches such as recurrent neural networks

When applied to metrics, time series models can learn what the expected range for the statistic is, and then detect if the statistic suddenly moves outside of the expected range. Some real-world examples can be found in Figure 2-3, where Airbnb uses time series metric monitoring on staged listings data.

This approach takes slightly less effort than setting a hard range for a statistic—the user need not estimate or enter the lower and/or upper bounds for the statistics. Sophisticated and well-calibrated time series models can adjust for a wide variety of factors, such as seasonality, holidays, and changes in trend or variance over time. Thus, the range the statistic is tested against shrinks, allowing the system to detect unexpected changes that might be missed with a wider static range while still minimizing false positive notifications.

We recommend using a time series approach to set the range for metrics in most cases. In situations where there is a very clear threshold that a metric should not cross, hand-coded ranges are still useful. For example, if the business has a service-level agreement (SLA) for responding to 95% of a customer's requests within four hours, then it's a good idea to set a hard bound on that statistic.

Automating Data Quality Monitoring with Unsupervised Machine Learning

Having covered the traditional (nonautomated) approaches to monitoring, it's time to introduce a new strategy: unsupervised machine learning. Data quality is no different from many other fields, where processes that were once entirely manual, like fraud detection, underwriting, and product recommendations, can now be handled by ML algorithms. These algorithms allow for far greater efficiency and can operate at a cadence and with a consistency that drives better business outcomes.

While we explore unsupervised ML in greater detail in Chapters 4 and 5, we'll give an overview here and explain the key role it plays in automating data quality monitoring at scale.

What Is Unsupervised Machine Learning?

Broadly, an ML algorithm can be categorized as either supervised or unsupervised. In supervised learning, the data that the model uses to learn is labeled by humans. Image classifiers often use supervised learning—a human shows a model thousands of images labeled as a tree, a cat, and so on, and the model then learns to recognize similar objects in new images. In unsupervised learning, the model does not have human labels—it just has the data, with all of that data's inherent patterns and relationships. The model learns from the data itself and interprets new inputs based on everything it has seen so far.

Supervised learning does not make practical sense as a strategy for data monitoring, as it requires humans to collect and label a large, diverse set of training data representing real-world data quality issues the model needs to reliably detect. Given how data differs wildly from table to table, not to mention from company to company, it would be onerous to collect enough labeled data to make supervised ML work well. This makes unsupervised learning the better fit for monitoring data quality. Assuming you've developed a model that works well, it can begin monitoring a dataset without any initial setup and continue to learn and adapt as the data changes. These algorithms can be tuned to detect deep, complex issues in the data, such as:

- The percentage of NULL values in a set of columns has increased.
- A specific segment of data (e.g., one country) has disappeared or is arriving with fewer records than expected.
- The distribution in a column changed significantly (e.g., the credit score distribution is skewing much higher than expected).
- The relationship between multiple columns has changed (e.g., these columns used to sum to equal one another, but now no longer do for a subset of records).

We've noticed that some data quality monitoring solutions claim to be doing "machine learning" but are really just relying on time series models to monitor many metrics. Depending on the technique used, a time series model might be using ML under the hood, but it's narrowly scoped to trying to predict the next metric value in a sequence. It cannot analyze the underlying data and will not discover data quality issues that do not directly affect the metric being monitored. In this book, we will use the term unsupervised learning to refer to the more expansive challenge of detecting unexpected changes in the entirety of a complex dataset.

One of the most powerful aspects of unsupervised ML is that it aims to understand changes in the relationships of data in the table as a whole. This is important because data in a table is usually highly interrelated.

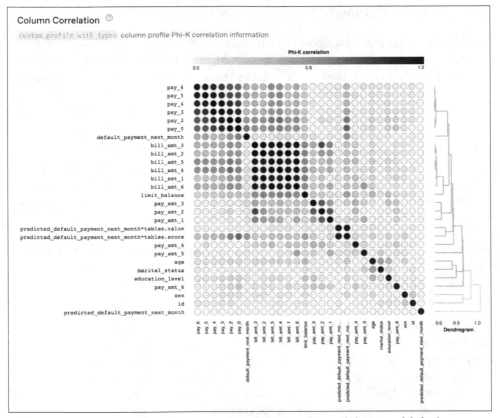

Figure 2-4. The relationships between columns in a credit card dataset of default payments from Taiwan (UCI Machine Learning Repository (https://oreil.ly/j6kw8)). See a full-sized version of this image at https://oreil.ly/adqm_2_5.

The credit card dataset shown in Figure 2-4 is a good real-world example. Each column appears on the vertical and horizontal axes, and the circles are colored based on the columns' phi-K correlations (*https://oreil.ly/VcXnJ*) with one another.[1] This reveals a great deal about the relationships between the columns in the dataset. Looking at the clusters of dark circles near the diagonal, you can see that all of the pay_N, bill_amt_N, and pay_amt_N columns are correlated with one another. There are more surprising relationships too. For example, age is strongly correlated with limit_balance and with marital_status. But marital_status is only weakly correlated with limit_balance.

When monitoring data for data quality, we tend to oversimplify things and consider just the values, distribution, or summary statistics in columns individually and create rules or metrics to monitor the column in isolation. But in practice, real-world data has all of the rich and complex correlation structure that we see in this credit card dataset. This has two significant implications for monitoring:

- If we monitor *every* column of this dataset in isolation with metrics or validation rules, then our monitors will also be very highly correlated. If the column correlations are causally linked to some data or process, then a change in that underlying mechanism may cause many dependent metrics to change, and validations to fail simultaneously. So, instead of getting one alert, we may well get dozens or more.

- If we evaluate each column for data quality in isolation, we disregard a tremendous amount of contextual information that could be very important for data quality. In the credit card example, if we suddenly found that age and limit_bal ance were less correlated, then this could signal a risk that one of the two columns has experienced a sudden data quality shock.

In order to fully leverage the rich structure of real-world datasets, avoid sending many alerts for correlated issues, and successfully automate data quality monitoring at scale, we need an approach to monitoring that can operate on the data arriving in a table as a whole rather than upon each column in isolation.

This is exactly what unsupervised ML algorithms are designed to do. Compared to more narrowly scoped metrics or validation rules, a good model will find a wider range of data quality issues, including unknown unknowns that humans didn't think to check for. It will automatically suppress repeated anomalies; on the second day that an issue recurs it will be able to use the first day as a "new normal" baseline. And issues that affect multiple columns can be clustered together and presented as a single

---

[1] The phi-K correlation is similar to traditional correlation methods (the Spearman or Pearson correlation) but can be used across data of varying types (numeric and categorical) and captures nonlinear relationships while behaving identically to the Pearson correlation for bivariate normal distributions.

issue; they're detected in one pass with the unsupervised algorithm and allocated to the appropriate columns and rows accordingly.

An Analogy: Lane Departure Warnings

Generated with DALL-E

When we thought about how data quality monitoring is being automated with ML, an analogy came to mind: how driving has evolved from an entirely manual practice to one assisted by ML algorithms. These algorithms are so valuable because they can account for a vast amount of context that may be too hidden, or too complex, for humans to capture via hard-coded, rules- and threshold-based logic.

Consider just one aspect of driving: ensuring that your vehicle stays in the lane and makes safe lane changes. If we applied the data quality methods we've discussed to this problem, we'd have something like the following:

The fully manual approach
> The driver simply pays attention to lane markings and never gets distracted or accidentally falls asleep at the wheel. This is how we have always ensured that vehicles stay within the lanes. It requires a great deal of attention and focus from the driver, and we still have accidents related to lane departures.

The system based on rules and metrics
> To picture an approach that relies on rules and metrics, think about trying to detect the lane lines on the road using a car-mounted camera and some basic statistics. If a certain percentage of the pixels arriving into the camera are yellow (essentially, a metric threshold), then the car would trigger a warning. This would be catastrophic, as many lane markings aren't yellow or solid or large enough to trigger this threshold. Plus, there will be many markings on roads (or other surfaces) that might appear yellow but have nothing to do with lane lines, causing false positives.

Additionally, there are many situations when drivers *should* cross over the lane line, such as when making a left turn or changing lanes to get around traffic or avoid an obstacle. In practice, this overly simplified system may lead to so many disruptive, unhelpful notifications that the driver disables the alerting mechanism in the vehicle—returning to the default case of having no notifications.

The ML approach

An ML approach to lane departure warnings would be more intelligent about whether or not to send the notification. It would use the context of the vehicle to avoid sending the notification if the turn signal is on—or if an object detection system notices that there is an obstruction in the way of the vehicle and that the vehicle should be departing from the lane. It could also prioritize alerting the user only if there is a high risk of encountering another vehicle or obstruction while crossing the lane.

This approach has the benefit of being far less noisy than the naive lane notification system and thus is much more likely to be listened to by the user. This dramatically increases the safety of the vehicle and the user's satisfaction while driving.

The Limits of Automation

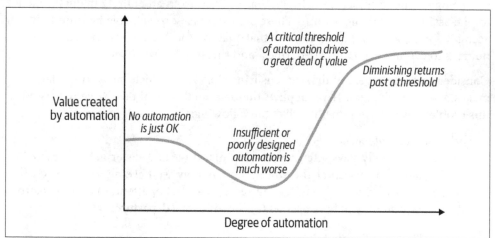

Figure 2-5. *Charting the value created by automation as the degree of automation increases.*

It's important to think carefully about the use cases for automation with ML. Poorly designed automation tends to be worse than no automation at all. That's why we've devoted a large portion of this book to developing a model that performs well on real-world data and avoids overwhelming your users with alerts.

As Figure 2-5 shows, there are also diminishing returns beyond a certain level of automation. Even if you have a powerful model in place, there will be problems that unsupervised ML can't solve. First, because it's sampling the data, it will never find a needle in the haystack like a validation rule can. For example, if you say a relationship must always be true between three columns, then if even a single record violates that constraint, a rule will find it—whereas it might simply not be sampled or significant in unsupervised learning.

Second, unsupervised models are by definition looking for new changes in the data and will never catch things that have historically always been wrong. For example, imagine that a column representing the number of vehicles owned by a customer was incorrectly coded at inception, such that missing values were coded as 0 instead of as NULL. This would cause downstream systems to think that many more customers owned zero vehicles than was true, when in fact, the data simply hadn't been collected for these customers. An unsupervised model or time series metric monitor would not catch this issue, because the relationships in the data have not changed over time.

And third, unsupervised models treat every column and every row as being equally important—and so may not pay as close attention to a given slice of the data as a metric that is defined directly on that data. For instance, if you're monitoring the percentage of times a column is equal to a value, then those records are much more influential in the metric outcome than they will be for an unsupervised monitoring approach that looks at the entirety of the table.

Automating rule and metric creation

A natural question regarding automation is whether it's a good idea to use algorithms to automate the creation of rules and metrics. While automatic rule and metrics monitoring is possible, it's very costly and leads to both false positives and false negatives (undetected issues).

Rules. Suppose you want to automatically create rules for your data quality monitoring system, rather than asking SMEs to specify rules by hand. You could start by predefining the common types of rules (uniqueness, NULL values, regular expression patterns, etc.) Then, you could sample some historical data to analyze. For each rule you'd defined up front, you could check each column in the table to determine if that rule is satisfied for sample data. Then you'd also need to check all the historical data to make sure that the rule continues to pass. Finally, you could productionize all the rules that passed on all the historical data. Great, right? Well, not exactly.

For tables with large volumes of data, the approach can be very expensive, as it ultimately requires evaluating every rule on every historical record to avoid situations where the rule will fail frequently in the future. For tables with small amounts of data, the rules will be very brittle—many may have passed only due to chance. And any time the data changes, you'll need to edit the rules or rerun the automated setup process. Finally, most of the really important rules that users want require customization with SQL so that they can be applied to only a subset of records in the table, or to express a complex relationship between columns or tables. And these customizations are very unlikely to be part of the predefined classes of rules in the system.

In practice, we have not seen this approach work in real-world situations. We recommend that you make it easy for end users to voluntarily add rules, using their own first-principles judgment, for situations where you need the data to be perfect. This has two advantages. First, the only rules that are created are the rules that really matter, reducing false positives and the number of rules you have to maintain over time. Second, if a new rule fails on the historical data, it becomes a learning opportunity. The end user might find and fix a historical data quality issue or learn something new about the structure of the data in uncovering *why* the rule fails.

Metrics. Automating metrics creation would mean that rather than asking that a user manually opt into the specific metrics they want to monitor, the system automatically computes and monitors a set of metrics for every table and column.

This would be easy enough to achieve. You could decide on the out-of-box metrics that you believe most users will care about. For tables, this might be the number of records per day and the time since the table was last updated. For columns, this might be the percentage of records that are NULL, zero, blank, or unique. Getting more sophisticated, you could configure each metric to only look for adverse events—a reduction in the number of rows, an increase in the number of NULL values, etc.

The approach of defining some metrics to automatically monitor ahead of time helps users get up and running with some insight into their tables' data quality right away, and it's a strategy we use at Anomalo. However, note that for even a small number of metrics, this solution can be quite expensive, as you'll need to do a significant amount of computation for every table and every column that needs to be monitored. Unless you have strategies for false positive suppression, it can also lead to alert fatigue—a single underlying data quality change might cause 10 columns to have NULL value increases, which will present as 10 separate alerts that a user has to triage.

While some metrics can be automated, we believe it's essential to give users the ability to define custom metrics as well. This ensures that important segments aren't missed, where there could be minor but critical changes to track. And it lets you capture the metrics that are most important to users—which often involve computing use case–specific statistics, like the percentage of records satisfying a multicolumn constraint, that would be excluded from an entirely automated approach.

A Four-Pillar Approach to Data Quality Monitoring

We've covered a wide range of monitoring strategies in this chapter. To recap, here are the different approaches an organization might take:

- Do nothing (yikes!).
- Implement data observability for your data warehouse (table stakes, but you aren't really monitoring data quality at all).
- Monitor a small subset of the data with handcrafted rules or metrics. This misses unknown unknowns (the issues you didn't know to check for) and covers only a fraction of the data.
- Monitor all the data using handcrafted rules and metrics. This is very expensive in setup and maintenance time, results in noisy alerts, and will also miss unknown unknowns.
- Automate monitoring with rules. This is extremely expensive, very brittle, and still misses tons of distribution and correlation issues.
- Automate monitoring with metrics. This is also extremely expensive, extremely noisy, and still misses tons of record-level issues.
- Automate with unsupervised monitoring only. While this provides good coverage, it can't catch everything and won't pay as close attention to critical data as handcrafted rules and metrics will.
- (Our recommendation) *Use a four-pillar approach.* You can implement data observability at low cost across your entire warehouse. Meanwhile, for data quality, automated unsupervised ML can provide a base level of coverage for obvious issues and unknown unknowns. Your platform should make it very easy for SMEs to augment automated monitoring with low-code validation rules and time series metric monitoring for the most important data and relationships.

Data observability, rule-based testing, metrics monitoring, and unsupervised ML can be used in combination to achieve the previously stated goals of *detect*, *alert*, *resolve*, and *scale*. This strategy gives you high coverage of real data quality risk while minimizing false positives and alert fatigue—all without having an army of analysts dedicated to the problem.

Figure 2-6 explains how the four components of this strategy balance each other's strengths and weaknesses. Figure 2-7 illustrates the capabilities of rules, metrics, and ML with some basic sample data.

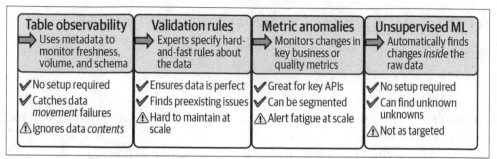

Table observability	Validation rules	Metric anomalies	Unsupervised ML
➡ Uses metadata to monitor freshness, volume, and schema	➡ Experts specify hard-and-fast rules about the data	➡ Monitors changes in key business or quality metrics	➡ Automatically finds changes *inside* the raw data
✔ No setup required ✔ Catches data *movement* failures ⚠ Ignores data *contents*	✔ Ensures data is perfect ✔ Finds preexisting issues ⚠ Hard to maintain at scale	✔ Great for key APIs ✔ Can be segmented ⚠ Alert fatigue at scale	✔ No setup required ✔ Can find unknown unknowns ⚠ Not as targeted

Figure 2-6. The four pillars of a comprehensive automated data quality solution.

order_date	order_id	order_state	order_amount
2023-01-01	6964352	CA	$143.50
2023-01-01	885358	CA	$17.65
2023-01-01	9056360	NY	$10.69
2023-01-01	5983636	NY	$84.69
...	...	...	...
2023-01-02	4130794	FL	$8.95
2023-01-02	1409193	NY	$61.42
2023-01-02	5391073	FL	$3.03
2023-01-02	298840	NY	$16.01
...	...	...	...

Rule: order_id is unique
order_amount ≥ 0
order_state is always in {CA, NY, FL}

Metric: the mean order_amount is between $30 and $40
the % change in number of customers per day is between -10% and +10%

Unsupervised: the percentage of records in CA has fallen sharply on 2023-01-02
there is a large increase in $1 order amounts on 2023-01-02

Figure 2-7. Examples of how different strategies can detect different types of changes in the data. Note that this is a simplified example, both in the data shown and the scope of issues detected.

The rest of this book is a guide to automating data quality monitoring at your organization following the four-pillar approach we've described here. We'll start by making sure that this approach is right for your organization and that the return on investment (ROI) would make sense for you and your data team. Then, we'll cover modeling strategies and trade-offs before moving on to key features such as notifications and integrations. We'll close by sharing how you can continue to maintain and grow your data health as your organization evolves.

## CHAPTER 3

Assessing the Business Impact of Automated Data Quality Monitoring

By automating data quality monitoring with machine learning, you can go beyond traditional approaches like metrics monitoring and rule-based testing. But before we get into the implementation details of this approach, we'd like to address what might be the elephant in the room (or, at least, on the page). *Is it worth it?*

We won't pretend that there's a single right answer to that question. Nor would we tell everyone to go out and build or buy an automated data quality monitoring platform tomorrow. However, what we can do is help you answer questions such as:

- What kind of data is best suited for automated data quality monitoring?
- What should our data stack look like before we invest in this?
- How can we measure the ROI of a new data quality monitoring approach?

Data quality issues are inevitable (see the following sidebar)—but the solution you choose is not. By the end of this chapter, you should have all the tools you need to perform a self-assessment of what your organization stands to gain from an automated approach. We'll cover the four key factors you should consider: your data, your industry, your data maturity, and how your stakeholders stand to benefit. Then, we'll provide insight into how you can assess the pros and cons with an ROI analysis.

"We Don't Have Data Quality Issues"

In Anomalo's early days, our founding team would talk to a wide variety of data and technology leaders to learn about their data stack, data quality issues, and needs. Occasionally we would hear from someone, "we don't have any data quality issues." This surprised us greatly.

As we dug deeper into this answer, we found that this only happens in one of two situations. Either nobody is using the data (and so the data quality issues are going undetected), or nobody is changing the systems generating the data (no growth, innovation, or third-party dependencies).

For example, while startups are finding product-market fit, they might not be using much data. This can be because they don't have a large enough sample size yet, because they are changing the product so rapidly that the data becomes obsolete, or because they are entirely focused on very large-scale design decisions that aren't easily informed by data. They may be collecting large amounts of data to support their ability to use it in the future—and they are almost certainly experiencing a large number of data quality issues. They just don't care yet.

On the other extreme, a well-established business that is no longer rapidly growing or innovating may have an application that is generating a large volume of data, but that is almost entirely static. They aren't upgrading the application or the technology that supports it and there aren't changes to operational processes. Such "hermetically sealed" systems are rare, but they are unlikely to experience data quality issues.

Assessing Your Data

Your data and its characteristics can tell you a lot about how (and if) automated data quality monitoring can meet your company's needs. Years ago, IBM introduced the idea of the "Four V's of Big Data": volume, variety, velocity, and veracity. It remains a useful framing, as shown in the original infographic (*https://oreil.ly/0kYP1*). Here's our interpretation of these four aspects and their implications for automated data quality monitoring.

Volume

If data is sufficiently small in volume, then humans can review it by hand. But even if there are just dozens of new records per day, that can merit automated data quality monitoring. As you approach millions or billions of rows per day, then the challenge becomes finding data quality issues in small, but important, segments of data—making it essential to invest in unsupervised learning models and notifications that avoid alert fatigue (aspects we'll discuss in future chapters).

Variety

The larger the variety of data an organization is capturing, the greater the surface area of risk for data quality issues. Sources of variety include:

- How the data is structured
- How the data is collected

- How time is measured in the data
- How the data is updated
- What entity is described in the data
- How records in the data relate to other records
- Variation in the business process being described
- How granular or summarized the data is

With different kinds of data, what you care about monitoring often changes. Consider, as an example, how columns can typically be categorized as either identifier columns, time columns, segment columns, or metric columns. Within each of those categories of data, there are different things you might care about monitoring—we've listed the most important ones here:

Identifier columns (e.g., customer ID)
    What to monitor: uniqueness, format, relational integrity

Time columns (e.g., event timestamp)
    What to monitor: granularity, sequencing, interarrival times

Segment columns (e.g., customer region)
    What to monitor: validity, distribution, cardinality

Metric columns (e.g., total daily orders)
    What to monitor: averages, distribution, outliers

A major aspect of variety in your data is *structure*. How structured your data is greatly affects the monitoring strategies that you might want to apply. With the right techniques, you can automate data quality monitoring even for unstructured data. But in general, the more structured the data is, the easier it will be to monitor with an automated approach.

Unstructured data

Unstructured data may include video, images, audio, and text files. When working with unstructured data, you'll need additional algorithms to "decode" its contents into values that you can monitor.

One approach is to compute metadata about unstructured data (e.g., the length of a video, the size of an image) and monitor that metadata for data quality issues. To monitor the data values more directly, you can train an ML classifier in some cases—for example, you could imagine training a computer vision model to detect blurry images.

Or, you might already have a deep learning model that uses the data as input, such as a model that learns to predict the next word in a sequence by ingesting a large volume of unstructured text. If you wanted to try to find issues in the input data, you could monitor the model's *embeddings*: N-dimensional numeric vectors that represent the input data. By monitoring for drift in the embeddings using an unsupervised ML approach, you can monitor changes in the input data by proxy.

However, every time the model is retrained, its embeddings will shift dramatically. So, this monitoring strategy is only useful with a static deep learning model. With the rise of foundation models (*https://oreil.ly/uy_Ci*),[1] which are large-scale deep learning models for text and image processing (such as DALL-E and GPT-4 from OpenAI), these embeddings are stable in between major version upgrades, and so monitoring how your unstructured data is changing in these embeddings spaces is a useful proposition.

Understanding the significance and impact of how your unstructured data is changing in embedding spaces remains a challenging problem. However, new break-throughs in the interpretability of individual neurons (*https://oreil.ly/nGEs_*) in these models may make this easier. In addition, organizations can associate their structured data with their unstructured data embeddings to characterize which segments of their data are experiencing significant shifts. For example, it might be the case that a significant distribution change was isolated to customers in a specific geography or to product experiences from a specific platform. Finally, you can always return to the text itself and examine samples that are unusual, and even ask a generative AI model to summarize a sample of these unusual records.

Semistructured data

Semistructured data doesn't have a fixed flat tabular structure; its structure may be nested and variable over time. But it does have a structure (such as tags and positional values) that enforces a certain hierarchy or relationship among its elements. To automate monitoring for semistructured data, you generally need a mix of schema validation, custom algorithms, and rules.

Many types of domain-specific data—such as geographic data or DNA sequencing—fall into this category. But by far the most common type of semistructured data is JSON data. Especially when a company is less mature, it's often easiest for engineers to store data as JSON: each record can have a custom schema to capture the idiosyncrasies of individual digital events or user profiles, and this schema can be rapidly changed over time, so there's no need to continually migrate (*https://oreil.ly/w2Dba*) structured data stores.

---

[1] Rishi Bommasani et al., "On the Opportunities and Risks of Foundation Models," July 12, 2022 https://arxiv.org/abs/2108.07258v3.

With JSON data, you'll need to consider how to monitor two concepts: *objects*, or *{"key": <value>}* pairs, and *arrays*, lists of values enclosed by brackets. In the most complex cases, you'll have nested combinations of both objects and arrays.

JSON objects can be easily expanded as additional columns in a given table of data. Suppose a column `json` contains the values {"name": "bob", "age": 32}. This column can be expanded into a string `json.name` column containing "bob" and an integer `json.age` column containing 32:

json [json]	json.name [string]	json.age [integer]
{"name: "bob," "age": 32}	"bob"	32

Some data warehouses will support this type of expansion automatically and help you enforce schemas for JSON. However, it's uncommon for you to know the schema ahead of time (as engineers on different teams will often be changing the schema or writing new ones). In this case, you need to take the extra step of expanding the data before you can monitor it.

JSON arrays are tougher to handle. You can think of them as a relational form of data that has been "compressed" into a single row. For example, an array might be used to specify a customer's addresses.

While you could expand these lists into a relational table, your options are not that attractive: you would need to expand each list into a new table with a customer ID column (repeated 1 to N times, depending on how many addresses each customer had) and address string column that contains the address information (essentially, doing database normalization), as shown here:

customer_id [integer]	address [string]
...	...

This would isolate this data from the other customer information, making it difficult to see correlations between address issues and other data issues, and would make it harder to root-cause the address issues using other customer information.

The alternative is to expand the address information into many columns (most of which will be sparse, as many users will have only a small number of addresses, but some may have many), as shown here. Neither of these situations lends itself well to monitoring with unsupervised ML:

customer.address1 [string]	customer.address2 [string]	...	customer.addressN [string]
...	...	...	...

One strategy for handling such lists of data is to randomly sample array elements and monitor these for data quality issues. This strategy also allows you to gracefully handle the cases where objects and arrays are nested. We'll discuss sampling in depth in Chapter 4.

Structured data

Structured, relational data is often the most important type of data to monitor, as it's the form factor most often consumed by analytics platforms, ML models, and other data products. While it may not be a large percentage of the total volume of data an organization amasses, it makes up a disproportionate amount of the *valuable* data. Within this category, there are three kinds of structured data you should consider monitoring: normalized relational data, fact tables, and summary tables.

Normalized relational data. In the context of data quality monitoring, you can think of normalized relational data as data distributed among multiple tables that all relate to one another (the exact definition and uses of database normalization are out of scope for this book). Each table will have a primary key and data that's uniquely associated with that primary key; each table may also have multiple foreign keys that can be used to join to other tables.

This type of data is very common in production applications. It's the most efficient way to store data when reading or writing to databases in an OLTP (Online Transactional Processing) mode, where each application interaction will generate DB reads and writes associated with it. Many data warehouses will copy normalized data directly into the data warehouse as a raw "replica" of the data being stored in the production application. Then, this data will be transformed into fact tables or summary data—the "data factory" work (see the section "Issues Inside the Data Factory" on page 7) that converts data into a more usable form for dashboards and other data products.

Data quality monitoring can and should be directly applied to normalized relational data, as this data is often at the "root" of issues that will appear downstream. However, this data presents only a limited surface for monitoring because each table is narrow and self-contained. To truly understand the scope and context of issues, data monitoring solutions will need to join to other tables in the relational model—which is expensive if done at query time.

Fact tables. To overcome the analytical challenges of having to write every query as a complex join and aggregation of multiple normalized tables, many organizations create "fact" tables, which denormalize data into a single materialized table.

For example, an ecommerce company might have a fact_orders table, where each row represents an order from a customer on their website. In addition to timestamps and identifiers associated with that specific order, it might also summarize information from other tables:

- Information about the actions the customer took leading up to the order (from a web/mobile events table)
- Information about the customer who placed the order (joined from a customer table)
- Information about the items purchased in the order (joined from an items table)
- Timestamps associated with the fulfillment, cancellation, or other processing of the order (joined from order processing event tables)

These tables are often the most insightful to monitor for data quality issues. Fact tables take very finely grained information, which might otherwise be spread across tens or hundreds of tables, and roll it up into an entity with real business value. They are also purpose-built and maintained to be a consolidated basis for other analytics, ML, and product teams to consume. As a result, issues visible at this level are usually important ones; they can be uncovered by a mix of unsupervised ML monitoring, rule-based testing, and metric monitoring. Fact tables also provide a great deal of context about each record in the table, which can help with understanding issues when they do occur.

Summary tables. Summary tables are aggregations of relational data or fact tables, often used to power dashboards and reports. For example, an ecommerce company might have a customer summary table that presents the latest statistics for each customer, like their number of orders, satisfaction rating, and expected lifetime value. Or a financial services company might maintain a daily aggregate of financial performance and risk information for key business segments that is used in generating financial reports.

These tables are important to monitor for data quality issues, as they are foundational for reporting applications. One wrinkle is that these tables will often show only the most recent information for each entity they are summarizing over. As such, data monitoring solutions need to take snapshots of these tables in order to detect issues that arise over time.

Velocity

Data is collected, aggregated, and distributed at a wide variety of velocities. Consider census data generated once per year, compared to transactional product data generated once per millisecond.

Table 3-1 shows that as the cadence of the data varies, so do the appropriate strategies for monitoring data quality issues.

Table 3-1. How monitoring strategies vary with data update cadence

Cadence	Scope	Example	Monitoring	Resolution
Year	Census	Large-scale population surveys	Manual	Manual
Quarter	Financial	Quarterly financial statements		
Month	Billing	Monthly billing cycle statements		
Week	Scheduling	Weekly scheduling data for retail	Algorithmic	Human review
Day	Summary	Daily user summary statistics		
Hour	Context	Medical device summary statistics		
Minute	Activity	Advertising attribution data	Deterministic	Programmatic
Second	Event	Fraud detection for online activity		
Millisecond	Transactional	Credit card approval process		

For data arriving less frequently than monthly, data quality monitoring is often a manual process. While ML models can be used to compare sets of data from one time period to the next, the problem is one of relevance. When data only arrives every year, a model needs years to learn about what changes to expect—and in the meantime, the processes that generate the data will almost certainly change, rendering the model's knowledge irrelevant.

For data arriving weekly, daily, or hourly, automated monitoring using unsupervised ML becomes possible and powerful. There is enough data history to train models, the sample sizes for evaluation are often large enough to detect meaningful differences, and the frequency is beginning to be too great to have humans manually review the data without significant cost and burden.

For data arriving as fast as every minute, or down to the millisecond, monitoring considerations change again. You need to be able to correct any issues in real time with a programmatic response—involving humans will be too slow. Therefore, while this type of data should be monitored automatically, more deterministic solutions are needed (i.e., rules-based testing only) so that there is no risk of false positives.

Veracity

The veracity of data is essentially the data's truthfulness or correctness. We can't ever *really* know if data accurately reflects the real world, so to get a good approximation of the veracity of a dataset, you can look at the inherent risk of new data quality issues being introduced (see Chapter 1). You can also account for factors that may increase your belief in the data's veracity—for example, a contract between data producers and data consumers that contains SLAs such as how often the data will be delivered.

The veracity of your data sources will obviously affect how much value you get out of data quality monitoring. We suggest reviewing Chapter 1 and the Appendix for examples of data quality issues and why they can occur, and mapping those issues to the types of data your business works with. You may also consider auditing the data quality issues you have had in the past: their number, severity, etc.

As a rule of thumb, the following data sources tend to be the least veracious:

- Data provided by third parties, though it can be very reliable, can also change unexpectedly without any communication with the consuming entities. This is often high-priority data to monitor.

- Data generated from very complex systems that are interacting with one another will be more likely to suffer data quality issues, as assumptions made in one system may not be respected by others.

- Data generated from systems that are undergoing continuous changes and rapid improvements are more likely to suffer data quality issues.

- Data generated by legacy systems is also more likely to have problems, as data quality tends to degrade over time, and often these systems are not being well-maintained.

Special Cases

In rare cases, some types of data are difficult to monitor with unsupervised ML. You may need a manual or purely rules-based approach in the following situations:

- Data where it's important to ensure that individual values are collected correctly at the point of entry, such as customer addresses that are entered manually. For this use case, you'd want a system to validate the data at the time of entry. If you don't detect the issue until it's in your data warehouse, you'll have a hard time getting it fixed unless you go back to the customer and ask them for the address again.

- Data with a very small number of entities or transactions. For example, data related to mergers and acquisitions at a financial firm would be hard to automatically monitor for data quality. There isn't likely to be a large amount of this data, and transactions will vary greatly in shape and structure.

- Data that's collected in a single large, static data dump. For example, consider data from a pharmaceutical trial. There may be an argument for data quality monitoring if the trial is running over a long period of time, but in most cases like these, the data is collected at once using the same process and system. If there are data quality issues, they are probably inherent in the data. You would need a validation rule to find such problems and to compare your expectation of reality with what the data says.

Assessing Your Industry

At Anomalo, our customers primarily come from the following industries: financial services, ecommerce, media, technology, real estate, and healthcare. While this landscape will certainly continue to change and evolve, we've done a great deal of thinking about why this is the case today. What makes the data quality imperative feel so urgent in certain industries?

It's partly due to the data factors discussed previously. All the industries mentioned work with large volumes of data from transactions and events. Some rely heavily on third-party data; real estate companies, for example, depend on multiple listing service (MLS) data, sourced from many partners with varying formats, timeliness, and quality. And in digitally native industries like ecommerce, technology, and media, platforms and products are undergoing frequent, rapid changes.

However, there are a few additional factors that can make a big difference in an industry moving to adopt automated data quality monitoring.

Regulatory Pressure

There's no doubt that regulations are pushing some organizations to invest in automated data quality. Financial institutions, for instance, must meet regulatory and supervision requirements with various market authorities or face significant repercussions. For example, Wells Fargo (*https://oreil.ly/-iddF*) received a $250 million fine and a legally binding consent order from the US Office of the Comptroller of the Currency in 2021 for failing to protect consumers from unsafe practices. Citibank was fined $400 million (*https://oreil.ly/nnIMz*) "related to deficiencies in enterprise-wide risk management, compliance risk management, data governance, and internal controls."

EDM Council (*https://oreil.ly/XVogi*) is a prominent global association that provides consultation and advice on enterprise data management and how it intersects with regulatory obligations (so don't go looking for music recommendations). Their Cloud Data Management Capabilities (CDMC) framework (*https://oreil.ly/BiFge*) provides best practices for working with sensitive data and is frequently used at financial organizations to ensure compliance. Key aspects of the framework include:

CDMC 1.1
> Automatically monitor key control compliance metrics and generate an alert when metrics fall below specific thresholds.

CDMC 1.2
> Ensure that the ownership field in a data catalog is populated for sensitive data that is migrated to or generated within the cloud, and alert customers with a triage workflow if a data asset is created that does not have this field populated.

CDMC 5.2

Data quality measurement must be enabled for sensitive data, with metrics distributed when available. Data quality metrics will enable data owners and data consumers to determine if data is fit for purpose. That information needs to be visible to both owners and data consumers:

- Automatically deliver data quality metrics to data owners and data consumers.

- Make data quality metrics available in the data catalog.

- Automatically alert data owners to data quality issues.

CDMC 6.0

Data lineage information must be available for all sensitive data. This must include, at a minimum, the source from which the data was ingested or in which it was created in a cloud environment.

It's difficult to imagine how these assurances could be put in place, at scale, without the techniques discussed in this book.

Even if there isn't this level of rigor in most industries today, regulations often start out in an isolated context with the most urgent cases and over time become a model for others. For instance, at one time, only hospital workers would regularly wash their hands, to protect ill patients; gradually, this began to include other groups like people who prepared food, and finally, it became common practice for everyone. Especially as the use of AI/ML grows, we imagine that data quality will only become increasingly regulated as it begins to impact more and more of our daily lives.

AI/ML Risks

As discussed in Chapter 1, AI/ML models will misbehave when the data that they are trained on doesn't match the data they use to make predictions in production. This can be difficult to debug, especially because a data quality issue often doesn't cause a model to completely break in an obvious way, but rather to perform worse for certain segments of users or scenarios.

If your organization is building models and, especially, if you're putting them in front of users, you've probably already invested significantly in data science, data engineering, and MLOps. This investment is at risk without automated data quality monitoring as part of your AI/ML stack. To illustrate why, let's take a deeper look at the problems that can happen due to data quality issues during model training and inference.

Feature shocks

Figure 3-1 shows a feature shock: a type of data shock that impacts a feature for an ML model. On a single day, the data for this feature has leaped far outside the historical norm. What effect will this have on a model?

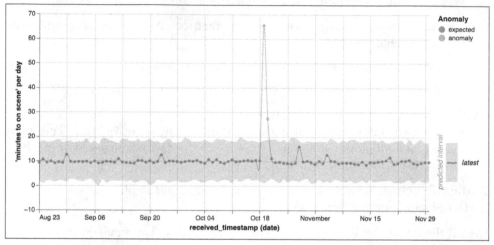

Figure 3-1. A feature shock in the data for an ML model. See a full-sized version of this image at https://oreil.ly/adqm_3_1.

If used in training data, this shock will cause the feature's importance to be dampened, as the model is led to believe that the feature is less reliable for making future predictions. If this kind of shock were to occur in production, your results would vary based on the type of model used.

Linear models, by definition, extrapolate linearly. So, if your feature shock is five times the expected value, then that feature will contribute a five times greater impact to the resulting score. Tree-based models are generally more resilient. A feature shock will tend to push the feature to the extreme end of the distribution. The model will then begin interpreting these values as being synonymous with whatever population was "normally" in the extreme.

Neural networks behave wildly under feature shocks. They have compounding nonlinearities in their architectures that can produce erratic behavior when data moves suddenly outside of the typical distribution. It can be almost impossible to predict how they will behave.

NULL increases

A spike in NULL values, in the best case, has the same effect on a model as a normal feature shock. But in the worst case, it can impact models in even more disastrous ways. If NULLs and zeros are treated the same way by the model, the spike could make the model believe there's been an increase in zero values, which may trigger unexpected behavior. Or, if the model aggregates feature values, you could end up with a problem where the NULLs compound.

Imagine you have a table with orders and items in the order, where a data quality issue causes one of every 10 item prices to be NULL. In some platforms, if you take the average of the item prices, those NULL values may dominate the aggregation, turning the `avg_item_price` field per order to NULL for any order that had more than one NULL item in it.

Change in correlation

Data quality issues can occasionally change the way that columns are correlated. For example, if there is a failure in how IDs are generated that causes a credit score dataset to improperly join to loan applications, then the resulting credit scores may be distributionally identical to the correct values, but they will not be associated with the correct loans. And so they will no longer correlate with other features of the data (age, income, credit history, etc.), and also will not correlate with future risk outcomes!

When there is a sudden change in correlation, the resulting behavior will depend on the type of model:

- Linear models can be very sensitive to the correlations of features, especially if they are not well regularized (a technique that prevents individual coefficients from being any larger than necessary to fit the data). In these cases, a change in correlation can cause a large shift in the model's predictions.
- Tree-based models are also very sensitive to correlations, as they operate by partitioning the data recursively one column at a time. A change in correlation will route records down entirely different paths, causing wild swings in the predictions.
- Neural networks will behave erratically, just as they will with feature shocks, as the distribution of the data suddenly begins arriving in a space (in the multivariate sense) where the model was not trained.

Duplicate data

Duplicate records can be a major problem for data scientists developing models. If data is duplicated by mistake while creating a training dataset, the model will "overfit" on the duplicated information, falsely believing that it's overrepresented in reality.

In training, an ML model learns to "fit" its parameters to the training dataset. However, it can actually do this too well if the model starts to learn the noise in the training data. This is called "overfitting." Achieving strong generalization performance (and avoiding both under- and overfitting) is one of the primary concerns of data scientists when building machine learning models.

Another place where duplication can cause significant issues is when splitting data for testing and training. Duplicated records can easily end up appearing in both the training and the test data. This will again enable the model to "overfit" the training data—in extreme cases, it can simply memorize the data, as the same exact records will appear in the test dataset. The result is the model will appear to have much better performance than it really does.

Data as a Product

When you sell or package data as your product, then the quality of your data is the quality of your product, making data quality monitoring more valuable to your business. Some companies directly provide data as a service. For a few examples, consider credit aggregators in financial services, MLS data aggregators in real estate, public company financial performance data in investing, and competitive price data in ecommerce.

In other industries, businesses aren't necessarily selling data, but their data is still an important part of their product offering. Consider how media platforms make data available to content creators. These creators need accurate metrics like view count and watch time to succeed at their work, which sustains the platform itself. If there's an issue in how this data is reported—maybe a bug causes double views to be logged for mobile users—it could cause significant repercussions for the business.

Assessing Your Data Maturity

As organizations develop and grow, they tend to move from an "immature" mode of just beginning to collect data, to a "mature" one of building AI and running advanced analytics. In her Medium article, our friend and advisor Monica Rogati summed this up as the "Data Science Hierarchy of Needs" (*https://oreil.ly/YmIce*). See Figure 3-2.

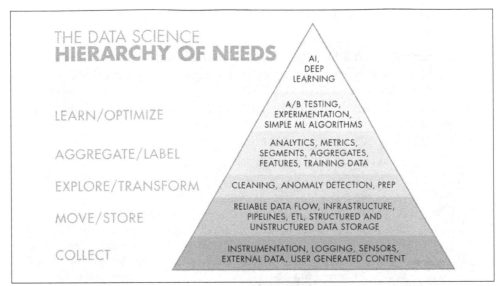

Figure 3-2. The data science hierarchy of needs (from Monica Rogati, "The AI Hierarchy of Needs," Medium (https://oreil.ly/YmIce), August 1, 2017).

In the early stages of data maturity, you start with data observability questions, ones that can be answered by monitoring table metadata. Did the data get ingested? When was it last updated?

When you continue up the pyramid and hit that middle layer where you start to explore and transform data, it's a good time to think about automating your data quality monitoring. At this stage, you've likely amassed a good amount of data, and you want to create a solid foundation for the next stages of aggregation and optimization. These future stages will rely on high-quality data in order to be effective.

Having reached the middle of the data maturity pyramid, businesses often feel they are missing the resources (analysts, data engineers, product engineers) to *fix* the data quality issues that they might find with more extensive monitoring. They thus reach the conclusion that they shouldn't invest in automated monitoring. However, we think this is a mistake. Those data quality issues are almost certainly disrupting the people they have today in the work they are doing and are building an ever-growing debt that will be very difficult to overcome.

Rather than avoiding knowing about the issues (and feeling obligated to fix them), you should build the muscle to identify issues and aggressively prioritize which ones you invest in fixing. Often, this means starting with a smaller number of missing critical tables (like fact tables) and agreeing up-front to criteria that must be met to warrant investing in fixes for data quality issues in those tables.

Unsure where you stand in terms of data maturity? Your data stack is a good indicator.

When a company hasn't adopted a cloud data warehouse yet, it often suggests that their use of the data they are collecting is still immature, and it's probably too early to invest in automating data quality monitoring. It's very hard to build a robust analytics reporting stack and data-driven team culture on top of production data stores or on data at rest in cloud storage.

 Some companies try to tackle data quality before they have invested in a modern cloud data warehouse, but this is typically a mistake.

Monitoring data directly in production databases (Oracle, SQL Server, PostgreSQL, etc.) can put heavy analytics loads on stores that were not meant to support these kinds of queries at scale, which often ends up affecting production traffic. Sometimes companies will try to monitor data quality in data at rest in cloud storage formats (Amazon S3, etc.), but without some platform to query this data directly, the best you can do is monitor the metadata of the files (size, format, date written, etc.). A common compromise is to set up a data lakehouse architecture so that data can be monitored on demand via query engines like Presto (or Amazon Athena, a hosted version of Presto) or Databricks (via Spark SQL). Data can also be monitored from a cloud data warehouse like BigQuery or Snowflake as external tables. However, each monitoring run will require reading the entirety of each file (modulo caching), so loading this data into a data warehouse can ultimately be much less expensive and far more performant.

Another indicator of data maturity is your organization's use of tools like Airflow, Databricks Workbench, and dbt to transform, aggregate, and enrich data in the data warehouse. The presence of these activities often suggests a need for data quality, as it introduces more risk of data quality issues being introduced. Additionally, these services often want to interact with data quality monitoring solutions via APIs in order to trigger data quality checks after data is transformed or published or wait to process data downstream if upstream sources are failing critical data quality checks.

Finally, a last indicator of maturity is whether your company has standardized on a data catalog. Data catalogs are useful when you have many stakeholders accessing a wide range of data; they help with identifying what data is most important. This is usually the data that should be monitored most closely for data quality. There's a synergy here, as well, because the results of data quality monitoring can be replicated to the data catalog and shown to users to help them understand if the data is well tested and of high quality.

Assessing Benefits to Stakeholders

As an organization moves up the pyramid of data needs, it tends to acquire a larger data team that demands more from a data quality monitoring solution. For example, a team of mostly engineers might be able to get away with just an API to monitor data quality, but as the number of nontechnical users grows, having a user interface to explore the data and communicate richer insights about discovered quality issues becomes increasingly valuable.

When determining if automated data quality monitoring is right for you, there's no better starting point than talking to your stakeholders directly. In the next sections, you'll find descriptions of how many roles in an organization can benefit from an automated solution and the types of features that are likely to be of interest to them.

Engineers

These are data engineers, analytics engineers, or members of the data platform team. They're in charge of managing platforms, ETL pipelines, and updating how data is tracked and stored. The kinds of data issues they care most about have to do with the freshness and volume of data in movement, and the reconciliation of data across different sources.

It's likely a team of engineers will be tasked with the technical implementation of a data quality monitoring platform. As such, they'll want something that's easy to configure, as automated as possible, and simple to integrate with other parts of your stack. Engineers tend to want a robust API that allows for one or more of the following options:

- Interacting with the API directly via code. This could be calling the endpoints directly, or via a Python package. This is the most flexible way of interacting with APIs, but not always the easiest.

- Using packages in orchestration platforms like Airflow and Databricks Workbench. These consolidate features in the underlying API and directly integrate them into the orchestration platform. Here's an example of the Anomalo Airflow operator (*https://oreil.ly/R7P36*).

- Interacting with configuration files (e.g., YAML, JSON) that are managed in a code versioning system (like Git) and are synchronized with the monitoring platform via API. This allows changes in configuration to be managed as code but isn't as flexible as calling the API directly.

Data Leadership

Managers of data teams typically want high-level analytics to be able to track the health of data quality as a whole, how it's trending over time, and how users are engaging in the platform.

Typical KPIs of interest to managers are:

Data quality coverage
> How many tables have checks defined? How are those checks performing? With a high-level view of coverage, leaders can pinpoint blind spots.

Data arrival times
> Leadership needs to be able to identify tables whose data doesn't arrive on time or meet SLAs.

Data quality trends
> A snapshot statistic is not enough to track data quality. It's essential that managers can track improvements over time with time series views and week-over-week changes.

Repeat offenders
> It's helpful if managers can get a list of tables that are the most problematic, or checks that fail the most often, to prioritize their next data quality initiatives.

For examples of how a data quality monitoring solution can provide tools for data leadership, see Figures 3-3 and 3-4.

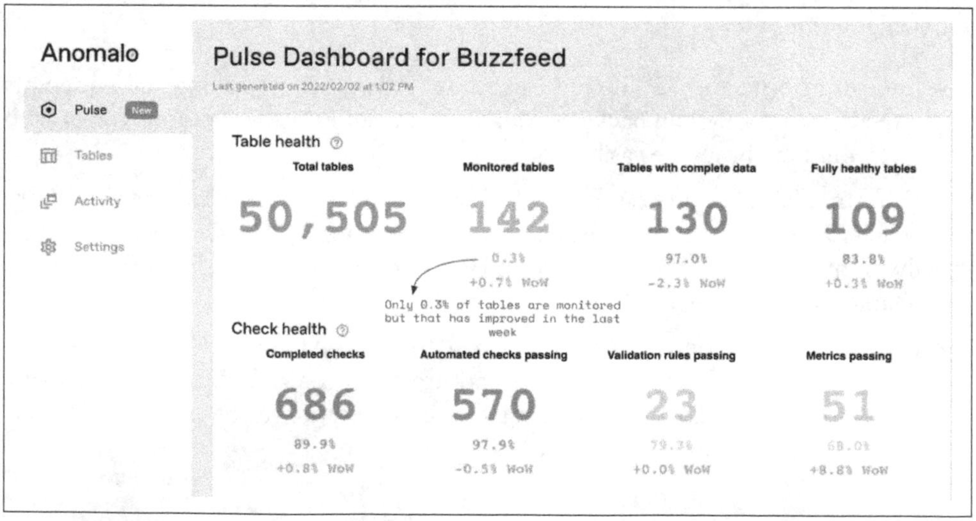

Figure 3-3. Anomalo's Pulse dashboard gives high-level statistics on data quality at an organization.

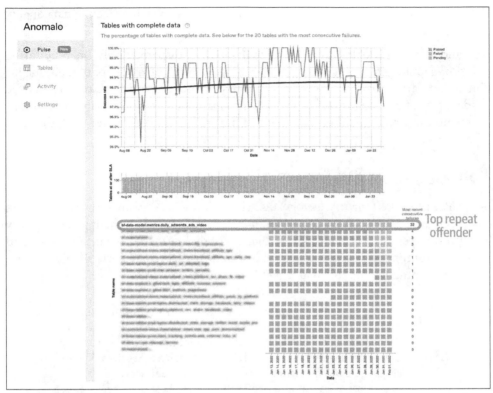

Figure 3-4. Clicking on any of the statistics provides trends in the data over time and identifies tables that are repeat offenders. See a full-sized version of this image at https:// oreil.ly/adqm_3_4.

Scientists

These are data analysts, data scientists, and members of the ML platform team who are involved in building data products and generating insights. They're typically interested in monitoring for missing data, duplicates, and distribution changes.

Unlike engineers, this group tends to prefer working with an easy-to-use UI, not an API. One way that automated data quality monitoring solutions can empower scientists is by offering them rich visualizations to explore data and determine the root cause of issues.

Consumers

This category encompasses everyone else who relies on the data products built by engineers and scientists to make decisions—such as product teams, operations, marketing, and compliance. These are often the deepest SMEs in the domains that the data is collected about and, as such, have a strong role to play in directing data quality monitoring and in triaging issues.

To build trust in the data and avoid a proliferation of disparate tools, the monitoring solution should provide this group with a single source of truth about data quality. Consumers are unlikely to be involved in issue resolution; rather, they should be made aware of data quality issues that might impact their work through notifications. These notifications should be clear, easy to understand, and delivered with the right level of urgency.

Conducting an ROI Analysis

After assessing the four key factors discussed—your data, your industry, your data maturity, and your stakeholders—you might decide that automating data quality monitoring seems like a good idea. In that case, you'll want to convince yourself and others by running an assessment of the likely ROI. Such an analysis should account for both quantitative and qualitative metrics.

For more details on conducting an ROI analysis beyond what's in this chapter, interested readers may want to review the case study (*https://oreil.ly/_K7lj*) by Prakash Jaganathan, Senior Director of Enterprise Data Platforms at Discover Financial Services. Discover's large suite of digital banking and payment services products is supported by hundreds of software applications that produce and persist petabytes of data. The case study tells the story of why, to innovate and excel in data quality, Discover addressed the fundamental challenges with traditional, deterministic data quality monitoring by subscribing to an automated data quality monitoring platform powered by machine learning.

Quantitative Measures

You can start an ROI analysis by looking at the frequency of data quality issues in your business. How often are they happening on a per-table basis? How much does each incident typically cost: in business interruption, investigation and resolution time, and other adverse customer or operational impacts? For every data quality issue you are aware of, how many are going *undetected* and yet still having an adverse impact on your operations?

Once you estimate this figure, you can multiply it by the expected number of issues per table per year, and the number of tables that are important to monitor. You can justify an automated data quality monitoring solution if its total cost can reduce the number and severity of these incidents, and their resulting cost.

In addition, look at the hours your team has spent on data quality–related tasks, and the amount you predict this would go down by automating data quality monitoring. Typical tasks include:

- Creation and maintenance of automated data checks
- Setting up notifications and alerting
- Investigation, exploration, and root cause analysis
- Monitoring key metrics over time

If you have historical statistics on these tasks, then you can calculate the likely number of hours you'll save by implementing automated data quality monitoring. These are hours that can give back to your team in terms of time and talent devoted to other projects. It's best if you can run a trial with a vendor to see, for example, how long it takes you to set up monitoring on the tables you care about. If you're building in-house, it can be difficult to get clear numbers ahead of time, but you can set a target that would make the investment worth it and keep that in mind as you build a proof of concept.

When speaking with customers, we're often asked to help estimate the total hours to configure tables for monitoring and triage alerts so that they can weigh this time against what they're spending today on data quality. It's useful to keep in mind that with an efficient monitoring platform, most of the data quality effort will be focused on a relatively small subset of important tables. In a data warehouse with 20,000 tables, we typically see a breakdown like the one in Table 3-2:

- 10,000 of the tables (50%) simply aren't interesting to monitor at all. Usually, these are temporary, intermediate, or one-off tables that may be deleted in the future.
- 9,000 tables are used in processing and should be monitored for data freshness and volume using metadata. We refer to this as table observability, and it has the advantage of being much cheaper than running ML models across the entire warehouse while providing a baseline level of data quality monitoring.
- There are 900 important team-specific tables where, in addition to table observability, the business wants deep data quality monitoring using automated ML models.
- On 90 key tables, they also want to set up validation rules and metrics to monitor for some unexpected changes.
- There may be 10 critical tables that, on top of all the other monitoring, must have many validation rules for record-level quality. These tend to be the essential fact tables for the business.

Table 3-2. Monitoring tables in a data warehouse

Type	Tables	Percent of total	Use	Configuration	Monitoring strategy	Hours to configure per table	Total hours to configure	Alert frequency per table	Total alerts per week	Triage minutes per alert	Triage hours per year
Temporary	10,000	50%	Staging, testing, or experimentation	No monitoring		0	0	Never		0	0
Processing	9,000	45%	Production pipelines to producing important datasets	Table observability	Automatically detect schema, freshness, and volume issues	0.01	90	0.5× per year	87	5	375
Important	900	5%	Raw data and team-specific datasets	Data quality	+ automatically detect missing, bad, duplicate, or anomalous data	0.2	180	1× per quarter	69	20	1,200
Key	90	0.5%	Fact and aggregate tables powering data products and decisions	Data quality	+ monitor metrics and/or segments for unexpected changes	8	720	1× per month	21	60	1,080
Critical	10	0.1%	Critical data elements and executive level monitoring	Data quality	+ enforce validation rules for record-level quality	40	400	1× per week	10	60	520
Total	20,000	100%					1,390				3,175

You'll also want to weigh the setup and operating costs of your solution, such as licensing, infrastructure, and computation. Note that an additional consideration for these costs may be how predictable the spend (and therefore your budget) will be.

Qualitative Measures

Some of the qualitative benefits of automating data quality monitoring are:

- Speeding up development cycles because you can catch production issues sooner after feature release
- Improving confidence with partners due to high test coverage, fewer errors, and faster response times
- Having an "audit trail" where you can document historical data checks and past performance of the data
- Democratizing data quality and improving collaboration and ownership, thus increasing employee productivity and satisfaction
- Improving the trust in your data and therefore the ROI of other data-related efforts

Qualitative disadvantages of automating data quality monitoring can include:

- Resistance to change; employees must acquire new skills
- Needing to develop new training and onboarding resources
- Potential security risks; for example, if you use a SaaS solution that isn't deployed in a virtual private cloud (VPC)
- (If you build in-house) Needing to maintain your solution over time and bear responsibility for outages
- The risk of false positive or information-poor notifications causing alert fatigue (On the other hand, alerts can come with rich context and visualizations that characterize the issue, identify the root cause, and help the user understand the potential severity of the issue. A UI can also provide the means to triage and resolve issues. All of these conveniences go a long way toward reducing alert fatigue.)

Ultimately, we see data leaders contemplate the value of improving data quality as a multiplier for the ROI of their entire data budget (technology and people). For example, consider an organization that is spending $30M per year on data technology and $70M per year on data professionals (fully loaded compensation). The organization is investing this $100M per year with an expectation of generating a significant return. For simplicity, let's suppose that is a 20% expected return. Then the value they expect to generate per year is $120M, through improved human decision making, improved operations and better customer experiences powered by ML and AI, and new data products that may be monetized directly.

If data quality could be significantly improved, then it could be reasonable to expect that value to increase by as much as 10%. This could happen because less time is wasted chasing down data quality issues, and so the people investment is more productive. Or it could happen because the quality of the decisions and ML models are higher, which directly translates into higher ROI.

The net effect would mean that the organization would generate $132M of value, for an additional $12M of value per year due to higher data quality.

In practice, while conducting rigorous ROI analyses may be necessary in some cases (especially to convince your finance or procurement functions of the need to invest in data quality), many of the large enterprises we work with don't even bother. The case for improving data quality can be so obvious and compelling that the question is less about ROI and more about speed.

Conclusion

To automate data quality monitoring at scale, you'll need to make a number of trade-offs. You'll need to invest in new technologies, introduce new processes, and commit to fixing new data quality issues you uncover.

We've built an automated data quality monitoring platform because we believe these trade-offs are valuable for many companies. Along the way, we've had many interactions with enterprises and teams that are excited about this solution. But we've also learned about the situations where the time wasn't right, or the fit wasn't there. In this chapter, we've tried to offer the complete picture of why you might benefit from automating data quality monitoring and, on the other hand, why it might not be the solution for you.

Excited about the ROI of an automated data quality monitoring platform? In the next few chapters, we'll provide the detailed guidance you need to take the next steps. From different modeling techniques and considerations to how you can deliver high-quality notifications, the most technical topics in the book are coming up next. Get out your notebooks, especially your data science notebooks, because it's time to dive into the implementation details.

## CHAPTER 4

Automating Data Quality Monitoring with Machine Learning

Machine learning is a statistical approach that, compared to rule-based testing and metrics monitoring, has many advantages: it's scalable, can detect unknown-unknown changes, and, at the risk of anthropomorphizing, it's smart. It can learn from prior inputs, use contextual information to minimize false positives, and actually understand your data better and better over time.

In the previous chapters, we've explored when and how automation with ML makes sense for your data quality monitoring strategy. Now it's time to explore the core mechanism: how you can train, develop, and use a model to detect data quality issues—and even explain aspects like their severity and where they occur in your data.

In this chapter, we'll explain which machine learning approach works best for data quality monitoring and show you the algorithm (series of steps) you can follow to implement this approach. We'll answer questions like how much data you should sample, and how to make the model's outputs explainable. It's important to caveat that following the steps here won't result in a model that's ready to monitor real-world data. In Chapter 5, we'll turn to the practical aspects of tuning and testing your system so that it functions reliably in an enterprise setting.

Requirements

There are many ML techniques you could potentially apply to a given problem. To figure out the right approach for your use case, it's essential to define the requirements upfront. We believe a model for data quality monitoring should have four characteristics: sensitivity, specificity, transparency, and scalability.

Sensitivity

Sensitivity is a measure of how well an ML model can detect true positives. To be effective, an algorithm should be able to detect a wide variety of data quality issues in real-world tabular data. A good benchmark is being able to detect changes that affect 1% or more of records.

In practice, we find that trying to detect changes that affect less than 1% of records produces a system that is simply too noisy. Even if the changes detected are statistically significant, there will be too many of them to triage and understand, especially when scaled to a large number of complex tables. Our experience has suggested that changes that affect 1% or more of records are significant *structural* changes in the data generation or transformation processes that could be major new shocks and scars.

To find changes smaller than 1%, you can either use deterministic approaches (like validation rules), or you can focus the ML on a subset of data by running the model on a view that queries just the most important records.

For example, a social media platform might track hundreds of different types of events in a single large event processing table. Running ML on the entirety of the table would catch gross issues with the format and structure of the most common types of events that are collected. But you could instead run the model on each of hundreds of event-specific subsets if you wanted to pay close attention to them all.

Specificity

The counterpart to sensitivity, specificity tells you how good the model is at *not triggering false positive alerts*. This is especially important in data quality monitoring, where alert fatigue can threaten the adoption and efficacy of the entire approach.

Typically, a monitoring system tends to over-alert for a few reasons. One reason can be seasonality—if there are patterns in the data that repeat daily, weekly, or annually, the data might look like it's changing, but it's not really changing in an unusual or unexpected way. The monitor will also be noisy if it isn't able to cluster correlated columns that are affected by the same data change. Or it could send false-positive alerts if it reviews too small a sample of data or evaluates the data over too small a time window. Additionally, there are some datasets that are much more "chaotic" than other datasets, and so the threshold for how sensitive a check should be needs to be calibrated to each dataset (and may need to evolve over time).

We'll explore how a model can learn and account for seasonality, correlations, and other challenges of real-world data in Chapter 5.

Transparency

When issues arise, the model should be transparent and help users understand and root cause issues. You might think that this doesn't have to do with the model itself—after all, any fancy visualizations and root-cause analysis will happen *after* a data issue is detected. But your options really do depend on the ML approach you use. Your model's architecture and implementation will dictate how much you'll be able to explain and attribute its predictions. For instance, some ML features might help improve accuracy but will be difficult to explain to users in the context of data quality.

Scalability

To run daily on potentially billions of rows in a data warehouse, your system must also scale—in human, storage, and computational cost. It should require no up-front configuration or retuning by administrators to run, as this would just create another form of handwritten rules, which we've already shown in Chapter 2 not to be a scalable solution. It should have a minimal query footprint on the data warehouse and be capable of executing quickly on inexpensive hardware outside of the warehouse. These constraints will affect many aspects of our modeling decisions, and we'll address ways of making the solution more scalable throughout this chapter.

Nonrequirements

Defining what a system does *not* need to do can be just as useful as defining what it should do. You may recall from Chapter 2 that an unsupervised ML model should be one part of a three-pillar data quality approach that also includes rule-based testing and metrics monitoring. That's because it's simply infeasible to expect automation to solve every data quality problem.

Here's a list of nonrequirements for our model:

- It doesn't need to identify individual records that are bad (that's what rule-based testing is for: when you need the data to be perfect). Instead, we expect it to look for structural changes in meaningful percentages of records.

- It's not required to process data in real time. Not only would real-time evaluation of an ML model for data quality detection be difficult to scale, but it could also be forced to evaluate individual records, which is not within our scope. Instead, we expect it to evaluate data in daily or hourly batches.

- We can't expect it to be able to tell if data was always corrupted—that's not how ML works, as the model must be trained on historical data. If that historical data is wrong, there's nothing we can do about it! That's why an ML approach should only be relied on to identify *new* changes in the data.

- We can't expect it to analyze data without some notion of time. The model will be tracking data over time to detect changes. If there's no timestamp built into the data itself, we'll need to develop other ways of identifying when the data was generated (more on this later).

Data Quality Monitoring Is Not Outlier Detection

As we wrap up our discussion of requirements for a data quality monitoring model, it's worth taking a moment to address a common confusion: the difference between outlier detection and data quality monitoring.

Outlier detection can be a useful way of understanding complex datasets. There are many ways to identify outliers, but one of the most scalable and flexible approaches is to use a variant of random forest (*https://oreil.ly/oAZd2*) called Isolation Forest (*https://oreil.ly/teNNd*) to identify rows of data that are far from the "center" of a multivariate distribution, as shown in Figure 4-1.

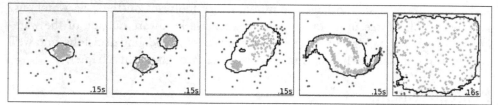

Figure 4-1. An example of using Isolation Forest in scikit-learn to find outlier observations (those points outside of the delineated clusters); from "Comparing Anomaly Detection Algorithms for Outlier Detection on Toy Datasets," Scikit-learn (https://oreil.ly/ rhJ9o).

Outlier detection can be accomplished with ML, and it seeks to find out about unusual aspects of the data. But the similarities with data quality monitoring stop there. After all, every dataset will have unusual observations—even a normal distribution has extreme values! These outliers may be interesting (they could be fraudulent records or just very rare events or data combinations), but they aren't necessarily going to be data quality issues, which can affect common or rare records with equal probability.

To identify data quality issues, we need to know when there is a sudden structural change in the distribution of data arriving into the table. We need to know if, in the past, records always appeared with a certain distribution, pattern, or relationship, and now, all of a sudden, that has changed in a significant way. On the other hand, every dataset has outliers. Outlier detection is solving a fundamentally different problem.

ML Approach and Algorithm

Now that we've covered the requirements, we'll share the approach that we recommend and the steps you can follow to implement it. We hesitate to claim that this is the only way to use ML to detect data quality issues, but we have yet to encounter an approach that more effectively meets the requirements in practice. As always, the devil is in the details. Things like feature engineering and parameter tuning/dampening make all the difference between an effective implementation and one that over- or under-alerts on real-world data, as we'll discuss further in Chapter 5.

Recall that we want to develop an ML model to detect unexpected changes in our data, without any humans labeling the data and telling us what constitutes a data quality issue. This makes this type of ML problem an *unsupervised learning* task. However, there does happen to be a feature of the data that we can use as if it were a human label, and that's the *time when the data arrived into the table.*

Unsupervised Versus Supervised: What's in a Name?

We've chosen to refer to the ML approach and model described in this book as *unsupervised*. This term conveys that we're attempting to identify which dates have anomalies in a given table *without relying on explicit human labels of anomalous dates.* When we leave it out, audiences often supply it: "Ah, so you're doing unsupervised learning."

However, we recognize that some might disagree with this classification. After all, each dataset used to train the model does technically have a label (the date), even if that label is not human generated, and so this could be considered a supervised model/process. As you'll learn in Chapter 5, we recommend fine-tuning the model by introducing anomalies that *are* explicitly labeled, so there's an argument to be made for the term *semisupervised* as well. As you read, please feel free to mentally substitute the term that you feel is most appropriate.

Herein lies the key insight in this approach. Every day, we take a snapshot of the data. Then, every day, we try to train a classifier to *predict whether the data is from today or not.*

Data

	listid	listtime	sellerid	numtickets	...	venuecity	venuestate	venueseats
Today	219247	2022-05-03 11:04:54	12619	4	...	New York City	NY	0
	17151	2022-05-03 15:27:17	27222	3	...	Washington	DC	0
	157318	2022-05-03 9:16:35	22899	9	...	New York City	NY	0
	75570	2022-05-03 7:05:29	44301	4	...	Redwood City	CA	0
	230809	2022-05-03 8:08:54	9683	4	...	Seattle	WA	0
	217754	2022-05-03 18:19:40	4999	6	...	New York City	NY	0
	7743	2022-05-03 19:36:02	4474	24	...	Green Bay	WI	72922
	39587	2022-05-03 14:13:25	37990	22	...	Baltimore	MD	48876
	...	...	...	...	...	...	...	...
	43729	2022-05-03 10:11:43	39835	4	...	Houston	TX	72000

	listid	listtime	sellerid	numtickets	...	venuecity	venuestate	venueseats
Yesterday	227155	2022-05-02 0:31:03	385	6	...	New York City	NY	0
	41479	2022-05-02 14:19:31	1674	8	...	Mountain View	CA	22000
	123523	2022-05-02 3:34:37	46271	8	...	Raleigh	NC	0
	11438	2022-05-02 11:20:46	38904	1	...	Dayton	OH	0
	118772	2022-05-02 9:51:39	41882	16	...	Kansas City	KS	0
	143671	2022-05-02 0:13:16	4554	14	...	New York City	NY	0
	101427	2022-05-02 17:26:38	3398	5	...	Philadelphia	PA	68532
	228561	2022-05-02 3:40:54	4975	3	...	New York City	NY	0
	...	...	...	...	...	...	...	...
	150082	2022-05-02 20:25:23	47888	18	...	Milwaukee	WI	0

Can we predict which day each record came from?

If there's nothing statistically remarkable about the data from today, then our attempt to train a classifier should fail—predicting whether the data is from today or not should be an impossible task, basically a flip of a coin!

On the other hand, if we *can* build a classifier that predicts with some accuracy whether a piece of data came from today, then we can be pretty sure that something is unusual about the data from today. And it's unusual in a meaningful way—because a few random changes in a couple of records aren't going to be enough to train a model to make a prediction one way or another. In fact, we'll even be able to use this method to say *how* significant the change is and set appropriate thresholds to avoid alert fatigue. By explaining the model's predictions, we can explain what's most likely going on inside the data.

A model can detect a change that's significant even if that change is not interesting. The most obvious example of this is when there is a date column. That column is going to change every day, and so it will always represent a dramatic change in the data! We'll cover how to handle cases like this in Chapter 5. The other kind of change that might not be meaningful is one that the end user simply doesn't care about. We'll talk about how to deal with alerts like these in Chapter 6.

Now that you have the main idea, let's explore each step in more detail:

Data sampling
How do you build a dataset to train your model and what is an appropriate sample size?

Feature encoding
How do you go from a row in one of your tables to a set of features that your model can use to make predictions?

Model development
What is the right model architecture for this algorithm and how should you train the model?

Model explainability
Once you've trained a model, how do you use it to explain a data quality issue?

Data Sampling

The starting point for building any model is to create a training dataset by sampling from your overall pool of data. For the algorithm we've just described, you'll need a robust set of randomly sampled data from both "today" (label = 1 for the class we are trying to predict) and "not today" (label = 0). The "not today" data should be a mix of prior time comparison periods: yesterday (or the last time you got a data update) for sudden changes, as well as other times of the week or year to control for seasonality (see the section "Seasonality" on page 91).

For instance, in Figure 4-2 we see an example dataset with 150k to 250k rows of data per day. A robust sample might include 10,000 rows from each of the following dates:

- 2021-01-16: the date you want to assess for data quality issues
- 2021-01-15: yesterday, which will help identify any sudden changes
- 2021-01-09: one week ago, to control for day-of-week seasonality
- 2021-01-02: two weeks ago, in case last week had anomalies

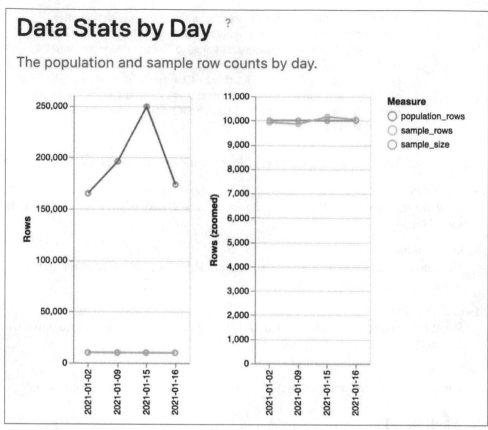

Data Stats by Day ?

The population and sample row counts by day.

Measure
- ○ population_rows
- ○ sample_rows
- ○ sample_size

Figure 4-2. Graph showing sample size compared to the entire size of the dataset.

Shadow Anomalies

If you compare a current date to a past date that had an anomaly, you might experience a phenomenon we call shadow anomalies. For example, imagine there was an outage last week where you lost records for a specific device type, like Android events. If you then compare today's data to data from last week, it might appear as though there's been a spike in Android events. But that's really just caused by the anomalous absence from last week! To protect against this, we need to sample from multiple different dates in the past (lookback dates) and/or we should exclude any dates that had very strong anomalies.

Sample size

In practice, we find that this algorithm needs at least 100 records per day to have a chance of finding meaningful changes in reasonably complex data. But that begs the question—what is the upper limit of the number of records that is useful for the algorithm?

Your sampling rate can be chosen to balance computational cost versus accuracy. We've run this algorithm against datasets that have as many as tens of billions of rows added per day. In practice, and based on rigorous testing, we've found that 10,000 records per day (if randomly sampled) provides enough data to capture most data quality issues, even those affecting as little as 1–5% of records. Quality improvement decays as sample sizes exceed 100,000.

Large sample sizes (say, 1,000,000 records per day) can be used, but the computational cost has not proven to be worth the value. A dataset would need to be very, very stable (little background chaos), and the change would need to be in a very small percentage of records (say, 0.1% of records), for this increase in sample size to be worthwhile.

It can seem like a mistake to sample a fixed sample size (10,000 records), rather than to sample, say, 10% of the data. After all, if I have 1 billion records, how can 10,000 still be representative of that huge population?

Perhaps counterintuitively, because the sample is chosen entirely at random, its accuracy doesn't depend on the total size of the data, just on the absolute sample size. For example, consider estimating the average income of a country. Just because China's population is 1.4 billion, and Luxembourg's population is 600k, does that mean that we would need to sample more people in China to get an estimate of the average income? No. In both cases, we could take 1,000 people and get a very good estimate of the average income.

Bias and efficiency

It is essential that the sample be taken *at random* from the table. If there is any bias in the sampling, then the algorithm will be able to find that bias and will represent it as a false positive change in the data that will confuse users.

It's also critical to ensure that the sampling is as efficient as possible. In practice, getting random records out of the data warehouse for the machine learning model is often the most expensive operation in this kind of a system. That is because the table may have billions or even trillions of records in it, and hundreds or thousands of columns. If a query naively required reading every record into memory or sending it over a network in order to sample, this would be disastrous for performance and incur a great deal of data warehouse costs.

Bias and efficiency can sometimes have a seesaw relationship. For example, one way of scaling random sampling efficiently in modern data warehouses is to use TABLESAM PLE operators rather than random() calls. The TABLESAMPLE operator is implemented in a way that allows the warehouse to efficiently sample random records during the query execution, without having to read the records into memory—but in some cases it can have negative trade-offs for bias.

In BigQuery, the TABLESAMPLE operator implementation (*https://oreil.ly/xVPqO*) works "by randomly selecting a percentage of data blocks from the table and reading all of the rows in the selected blocks." The documentation continues by explaining that, typically, "BigQuery splits tables or table partitions into blocks if they are larger than about 1 GB." This means that, in practice, the results returned by the TABLESAMPLE operator will often not be random in BigQuery and may instead be entirely in a single partition. If you've partitioned your data on an identifier that you use frequently for joins—say, a customer ID—then you'll have specific subsets of customers that will be far more likely to appear in your random sample than others will. This could meaningfully bias the results of your ML, causing you to continually see a shift in the user population over time that is entirely due to the sampling implementation rather than any real drift in your data itself.

So, how do you sample efficiently and avoid bias? Here are our recommendations:

- Ensure that you are only using a small number of days' worth of data each time you run the algorithm. These days can be stored as snapshots so that they don't have to be queried again (though it may be worthwhile to query them again, as the historical data in the table could have changed).

- Ensure that the table is partitioned on the date column that you are using to select the data. This allows the data warehouse to efficiently navigate to just the files on disk that represent these days and read and process only those dates of data without having to access other, irrelevant dates.

- Use the TABLESAMPLE operator to efficiently sample an approximate random sample that is larger than the one you need (e.g., if you need 0.3%, then sample 1%). Often the lower bound percentage that can be sampled with this operator is 1%, though the implementation varies by warehouse. Note that not all databases or data warehouses support TABLESAMPLE in a robust way—see the previous paragraph on BigQuery.

- Count the total number of records that you will have on the dates you are querying, in order to understand the exact sample percentage that you will need to query for.

- Take the final random sample using code that looks like: random() <= X for some X that gives you approximately the correct number of rows on each date after the TABLESAMPLE operation. This is far more efficient than something that looks like order by random() limit 10,000, which would require loading all of the data into memory in a master node in the warehouse and sorting it by a random number before applying a limit. The benefit of the random() <= X approach is that it can be applied in a distributed fashion in the warehouse in each of the worker compute nodes. Note that the minor downside is that your random sample is unlikely to be exactly 10,000 rows but will instead be a number that is quite close.

Another important consideration when querying for data is to ensure that the `WHERE` SQL filter is implemented efficiently. For example, for a table with the date column `created_date`, specified as a string in YYYY-MM-DD format, this would be very inefficient:

```
WHERE cast(created_date as date) = cast('2023-06-01' as date)
```

This code would require the database to read every partition and convert the `created_date` column in memory in order to decide if the record should be included.

Instead, try:

```
WHERE created_date = '2023-06-01'
```

Now the data warehouse can use metadata about each partition to decide which to exclude entirely from being considered by the query. This can be quite challenging for tables that are formatted with unusual date or time partitions. At Anomalo, we have had to add support for all of the types in Figure 4-3.

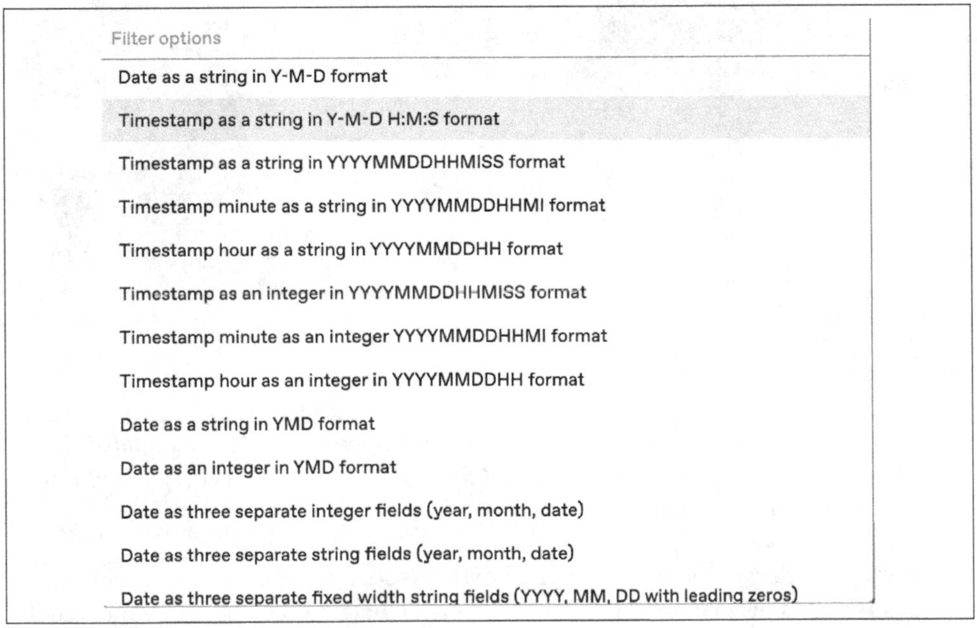

Filter options

Date as a string in Y-M-D format

Timestamp as a string in Y-M-D H:M:S format

Timestamp as a string in YYYYMMDDHHMISS format

Timestamp minute as a string in YYYYMMDDHHMI format

Timestamp hour as a string in YYYYMMDDHH format

Timestamp as an integer in YYYYMMDDHHMISS format

Timestamp minute as an integer YYYYMMDDHHMI format

Timestamp hour as an integer in YYYYMMDDHH format

Date as a string in YMD format

Date as an integer in YMD format

Date as three separate integer fields (year, month, date)

Date as three separate string fields (year, month, date)

Date as three separate fixed width string fields (YYYY, MM, DD with leading zeros)

Figure 4-3. Example of types of date/time partitions.

Jeremy has been known, at times, to joke that we expect to support time in "number of days since Kevin Bacon was born" format soon.

Feature Encoding

ML models aren't typically trained on raw data, but rather they learn using numerical features, which are transformations of the raw data into signals the model can use. How the raw data is transformed can have a significant impact on the performance of the model and typically requires both expertise in ML and subject matter expertise in the data and problem at hand. This process, called feature engineering, must be fully automated in our anomaly detection algorithm.

How this works is as follows: each record in the sample will have a number of columns, and each column could be an integer, float, string, Boolean, date or timestamp, or complex type like JSON or an array. You'll need an automated process that walks through each column (expanding complex types like JSON into subcolumns if necessary—see "Semistructured data" on page 44 for more on this), extracts information that could be interesting to your model, and encodes this information into a floating point matrix of ML features.

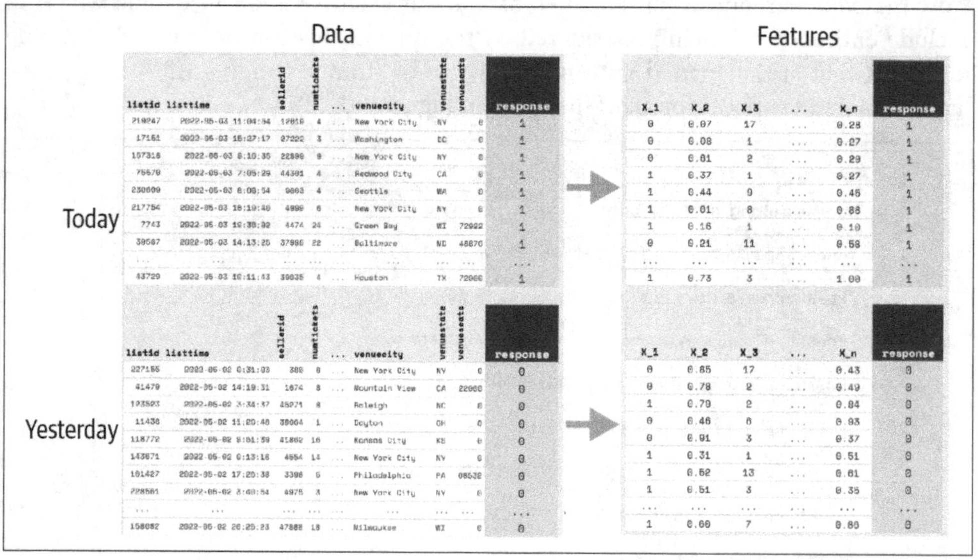

Figure 4-4. Encoding data as features. Note that the response variable (a.k.a label) corresponds to the date: 0 for yesterday and 1 for today. See a full-sized version of this image at https://oreil.ly/adqm_4_4.

You'll want to develop a library of candidate encoder types to apply, based on the features that you believe could tell you whether the data has changed in a meaningful way (see Figure 4-4). Here are some encoders we recommend:

Numeric

Converts Boolean, integer, and floating values into floats

Frequency

How often each value appears in the sample of data

IsNull

A binary indicator for whether the column is NULL

TimeDelta

Seconds between a time and when the record was created

SecondOfDay

The time of day the record was created

OneHot

A one-hot encoder, which lets you map feature values (like categories or frequent integer values) to a binary yes or no indicator variable for each unique value in the column

Data scientists may wonder about the applicability of common encoders like term frequency-inverse document frequency (TF-IDF), mean encoding, or Laplace smoothing. Many standard encoders aren't very relevant for tree-based models (log transformation, mean encoding, principal component analysis [PCA]). Others would require a lot of subject matter expertise about the specific data to use well (Laplace smoothing), and still others might be useful but would be very hard to interpret (TF-IDF, word/vector embeddings).

You have to be careful with how complex you make your encoders, because in the end, you'll need to use these encodings to explain the data quality issue to the user. For example, we tested a "gap" encoder for time, integer, and numeric fields, which took each observation and computed the gap between it and the next largest value in that column. In practice, this was able to detect some kinds of data quality issues, but it would also detect many other changes in the data that would be both hard to understand and/or irrelevant for our purposes—like changes in the grain of how data is being logged or unrelated changes in the volume (and therefore density) of observations.

Model Development

To meet the scalability requirements and work in a practical setting, you need a model architecture that's fast at inference and training, can be trained on relatively small samples, and will generalize to any kind of tabular data (when properly feature-encoded). Gradient-boosted decision trees work well for this use case, and you'll find libraries like XGBoost (*https://oreil.ly/_KZPk*) readily available for model development.

Gradient-boosted decision trees work in an iterative fashion by building a sequence of decision trees on the dataset, where each tree (or "step") is designed to correct the mistakes of all of the trees that came before it. Ultimately, the model's prediction takes into account the results from all the trees that were trained at each step (this is known as an ensemble model). See Figure 4-5.

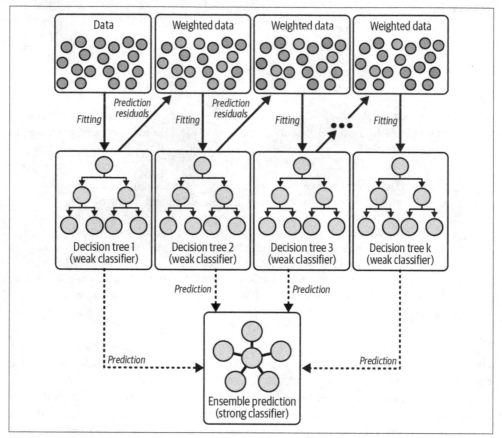

Figure 4-5. A gradient-boosted decision tree (adapted from Haowen Deng et al., "Ensemble Learning for the Early Prediction of Neonatal Jaundice with Genetic Features," BMC Medical Informatics and Decision Making 21, no. 338 [2021]).

Helpfully, gradient-boosted decision trees have a very small number of parameters that really matter for tuning (mainly, the learning rate and the complexity of each tree, though there are others) and can be trained on datasets with thousands or even millions of records very quickly.

Some alternate approaches, such as linear models, are too simple to learn the complex patterns in most structured datasets. Other approaches, like neural networks, are often too complex for problems like this and require extremely large volumes of heterogeneous data to become very powerful (as in image and language models).

The downside of gradient-boosted decision trees, like any structured ML technique, is that they require feature engineering: human experts have to tell the model what aspects of the data it should consider when making its predictions, and this can take a lot of time and energy.

Do You Really Need ML for This?

Here's a question: Instead of using an ML model, why not just evaluate differences in the distribution of each column separately from one another? Well, in practice, you'll still need an approach that can evaluate each column in nonlinear ways, and as we will see in Chapter 5, it's important to control for column correlations. A multivariate model like gradient boosting decision trees allows us to learn about all of the columns simultaneously and their nonlinear relationships. And explainability algorithms like Shapley (SHAP) values allow you to explain this model as clearly as you could a collection of column-based comparisons.

Training and evaluation

In theory, gradient-boosted decision trees could continue iterating and iterating endlessly, so it's essential to cap the number of steps at some limit. To do this, you'll typically want to evaluate the model's performance after each step. Select a random portion of your data to use as a holdout set for evaluation (and not training) and test the model after each iteration. Your model's performance will be an indication of whether there is something anomalous about today's data.

Specifically, there are three model performance patterns that we tend to see in practice shown in Figure 4-6. On these charts, the x-axis represents the number of trees added to the model (the number of iterations), while the y-axis plots a measure of the model's accuracy (the log of the loss function). Note that here, the y-axis is technically plotting how much "error" there is in the model's predictions, so a lower value indicates higher accuracy.

The first scenario, "No anomaly," is when there is little progress made on the training data and the performance on the test data begins getting worse very quickly. This means that there is unlikely to be any anomaly in the new data.

The second scenario, "Incomplete," happens when the model doesn't have enough time to converge. You reach a maximum number of trees (set to prevent the model from running indefinitely) and yet still find that the training error and test error are declining. You'll either need to add more trees or, perhaps more prudently, increase the learning rate, which causes the gradient boosting algorithm to take larger "steps" in the direction of each tree that it evaluates.

The third scenario, "Optimal," occurs when the model makes good progress on training and test, until a point where the test loss begins increasing. This indicates that you can stop where the test loss was at its minimum. At that point, the model will have learned as much about what differentiates these two datasets as it can, given the other parameters of the learning algorithm.

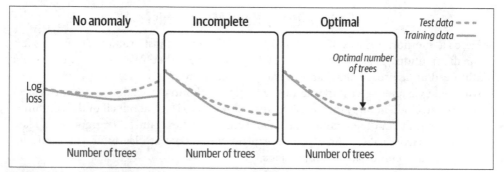

Figure 4-6. The three most common scenarios encountered when plotting the model's performance on training and test data as the number of trees increases. Performance is measured using a log loss error function (a lower value on the y-axis indicates better performance).

In practice, in order to provide consistently interpretable model statistics and explainability results, you'll need to strike a balance between optimizing your model for a single dataset and building a model that generalizes to many datasets across different periods of time.

Computational efficiency

Many organizations have important tables that can include billions of records. Examples include:

- Transactional data from financial services industries
- Raw event data from high-traffic applications or websites
- Digital advertising impression and event-level data
- Physical sensor data
- Messaging information from social platforms

With data at this scale, it's easy to create a monitoring strategy that will be cost-prohibitive, or simply fail to successfully run even with modern data warehouses.

Because we've placed a limit on the number of records we are sampling per day, most of the computation and memory usage in the model will scale linearly with the number of columns added. For example, searching for the best split while expanding a decision tree at each node will increase linearly with the number of columns you need to search over. Although typical tables have 10–50 columns, it's common for tables to have 200 columns, and some tables have thousands. Furthermore, tables may have JSON data that you'll need to automatically expand into new synthetic columns, which can lead to tables with 10,000 columns in some situations.

The following optimizations can make your algorithm more computationally efficient:

- Ensuring that you are only querying for one day of data at a time and snapshotting results as much as possible to build history. Note that this comes at a cost, as algorithms will have less history to work with on day one and won't be as effective in a "cold start" scenario.

- Randomly sampling records from the table using the data warehouse (using the efficient techniques noted earlier in "Bias and efficiency" on page 73) and computing more complex profiling or ML results on the random samples.

- If using gradient boosting decision trees, limit the depth and total number of trees, as we are not typically looking for very complex interactions, and early stop if your test error increases significantly during the training process.

- Optimize the learning process itself, which, depending on your computing platform and learning algorithm, could include steps like using sparse encodings, distributing learning via multiprocessing, or utilizing GPUs.

Model Explainability

If you have a model that performs well on the test set, this indicates that you've found a potential data quality issue. The next step is to explain what the model has found.

Explainability is key for several reasons. First, it tells you *how* anomalous the data from today is. This lets you perform many kinds of tuning to avoid alert fatigue (more on this in Chapters 5 and 6). For those issues where you do fire an alert, knowing the severity will help end users prioritize their response.

Second, explainability tells you *where* in the data that anomaly is located. This lets you point investigators to the right segments of the data and create all kinds of interesting root cause analysis aids, like samples of bad data (more details in Chapter 6).

So how does model explainability work? The idea is to derive a score that credits how much each individual {row, column} cell in the dataset contributed to the model's prediction. While there are several approaches, we use SHAP (*https://oreil.ly/TdiVx*), which essentially approximate a local linear estimation of what the algorithm is doing for each cell in the dataset.

To see how this works in practice, suppose that we are trying to detect data quality issues in a table of credit card transaction data and have sampled 10,000 records from yesterday and today, encoded our features, and built our model predicting on which day each record arrived. Then let's follow the following four records through the SHAP explainability process:

Amount	Type	FICO score	Brand	Type	Credit limit	Source
$18	Swipe	684	Discover	Debit	$12,564	Today
$59	Chip	578	Mastercard	Credit	$7,600	Today
−$445	Chip	689	Visa	Credit	$6,700	Yesterday
$137	Chip	734	Mastercard	Credit	$7,100	Yesterday

In this case, we have two records from yesterday and two records from today. (Recall that the source column isn't used to make predictions about which day the data arrived on; rather, it is the response that we are training the model to predict.)

Then, suppose that we take our model and make predictions for each row for which day we think it is likely to have arrived on:

Amount	Type	FICO score	Brand	Type	Credit limit	Source	Predicted Pr(Today)
$18	Swipe	684	Discover	Debit	$12,564	Today	51%
$59	Chip	578	Mastercard	Credit	$7,600	Today	78%
−$445	Chip	689	Visa	Credit	$6,700	Yesterday	45%
$137	Chip	734	Mastercard	Credit	$7,100	Yesterday	52%

In this case, we find that our model thinks there is a 78% chance that the second record is from today, whereas the other three records are within ±5% of the 50% average prediction that would indicate the model has no strong bias for which day the data came from.

Rather than working directly with the predicted probability (which is hard to express as a linear relationship, given probabilities are naturally bounded between 0% and 100%), we convert the probabilities into their log odds, using the formula `log odds = ln [ probability / (1 - probability) ]`:

Amount	Type	FICO score	Brand	Type	Credit limit	Source	Predicted Pr(Today)	Log odds
$18	Swipe	684	Discover	Debit	$12,564	Today	51%	0.02
$59	Chip	578	Mastercard	Credit	$7,600	Today	78%	0.55
−$445	Chip	689	Visa	Credit	$6,700	Yesterday	45%	−0.09
$137	Chip	734	Mastercard	Credit	$7,100	Yesterday	52%	0.03

Then, we can run the SHAP algorithm, which will decompose these log odds statistics into a linear combination of contributions from each of the columns as used in the ML model (in reality, we would need to get the SHAP values at the feature level, and then aggregate those, but you get the point):

Amount	Type	FICO score	Brand	Type	Credit limit	Predicted Pr(Today)	Predicted Pr(Today)	Log odds
0.01	0.02	0.02	−0.01	0.00	−0.01	Today	51%	0.02
−0.03	0.01	0.41	0.19	−0.01	−0.03	Today	78%	0.55
0.02	−0.03	−0.05	0.02	−0.03	−0.02	Yesterday	45%	−0.09
0.01	−0.02	−0.01	0.01	0.02	0.02	Yesterday	52%	0.03

In this case, we find that the FICO SCORE and BRAND column values are contributing significantly to the model's prediction that the second record is from today. Examining the data values above, we see that this corresponds to:

- FICO SCORE = 578
- BRAND = 'Mastercard'

This suggests that there may be something anomalous happening with the distribution of low credit scores for Mastercard transactions (though we are examining only a few records here—in practice, we would look at the SHAP values distribution summarized across all 10,000 records per day).

After normalizing and appropriately tuning the SHAP values following techniques in Chapter 5, the end result is what we call the "anomaly score." Importantly, this score can be aggregated and/or sliced to provide many different levels of granularity.

At the lowest level, you can look at the anomaly score for *each individual {row, column} cell in the sampled data*. From here, you can aggregate the anomaly scores for a row to find the most anomalous entries, or by sets of rows to find anomalous segments. You can take the average anomaly score by column to find the most anomalous columns. Or you can calculate the anomaly score for the entire table. You can also cluster anomaly scores to find correlations across columns (more on this in Chapter 5).

Knowing the anomaly score isn't only important for data where there's been a significant change. By calculating the score for every record in the table, you can create visualizations that put the anomaly in context, as in Figure 4-7.

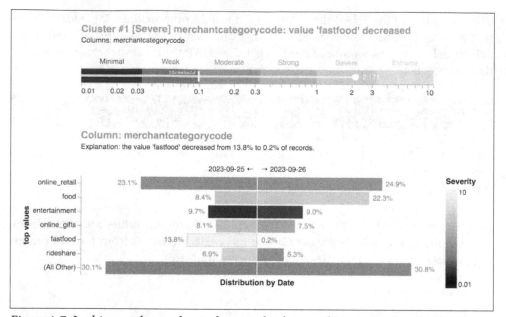

Figure 4-7. In this sample merchants dataset, the data quality monitoring platform has detected an issue where the value fastfood *has decreased significantly in the column* merchantcategorycode. *The anomaly score is compared to the anomaly score for other values in this table. You can see that there was simultaneously a significant increase in the value* food. *These two changes may be related, as suddenly* fastfood *records were misclassified as simply* food. *See a full-sized version of this image at https://oreil.ly/adqm_4_7.*

As you can see in Figure 4-7, you can assign human-readable categories to anomaly scores to help with interpretation. Based on our experience working with a wide variety of datasets, we group anomaly scores into six different buckets, from minimal to extreme. These categories are based on the log of the overall anomaly score—every two buckets represents an order of magnitude increase in the score:

Minimal
> There is little to no significant change in the data.

Weak
> A small percentage of the data is affected by a change that requires explanation and careful study to detect.

Moderate
> A small percentage of the data is affected by an obvious change, or a moderate percentage is affected by a change that requires simple explanation.

Strong

A significant percentage of the data is affected by an obvious change, or a majority of the data is affected by a change that is easily explained (though it may not be obvious at first glance).

Severe

A majority of the data is subject to a change that is obvious.

Extreme

There is a change that is obviously affecting almost the entirety of the data from today.

You may notice a threshold in Figure 4-7—it's important to use the anomaly score for each table to learn a custom threshold for when to trigger an alert, as the data in some tables changes more frequently than in others. We'll discuss this in Chapter 5.

Putting It Together with Pseudocode

The following Python pseudocode gives an example of how you could apply the approach described in this chapter to find anomalies between two days of data and summarize them by column. Don't take this code too literally though; it is meant to simply illustrate the concepts and how they fit together at a high level. In particular, note that this ignores more complex issues like seasonality, multiple lookbacks, and correlated features and doesn't implement the sampling, feature engineering, or anomaly score computation pieces in any detail.

```python
# General imports
import pandas as pd
import datetime as dt
import xgboost as xgb
from sklearn.model_selection import train_test_split
from shap import TreeExplainer

# Import hypothetical sub-modules that perform more detailed tasks
from data_access import query_random_sample
from feature_engineering import determine_features, encode_feature
from explainability import compute_column_scores

def detect_anomalies(
        table: str,
        time_column: str,
        current_date: dt.date,
        prior_date: dt.date,
        sample_size: int
    ) -> dict[str, float]:
```

Here we are defining a method in pseudocode that will detect anomalies in data by comparing samples from two different dates, training a model, and computing anomaly scores.

It accepts the following as parameters:

table
> the name of the table to query

time_column
> the name of the time column used to filter the data

current_date
> the current date for which to sample data

prior_date
> the prior date for which to sample data

sample_size
> the number of rows to randomly sample for each date

It returns a dictionary where each key is a column name and each value is the column's anomaly score.

The next piece of the pseudocode implements the body of the method and takes us from the data sampling step all the way through to explaining the model's predictions:

```
# Obtain random samples of data for the specified dates
data_current = query_random_sample(
    table, time_column, current_date, sample_size)
data_prior = query_random_sample(
    table, time_column, prior_date, sample_size)

# Create a binary response variable indicating the date
y = [1] * len(data_current) + [0] * len(data_prior)

# Concatenate the data, ensuring the order of concatenation
data_all = pd.concat([data_current, data_prior], ignore_index=True)

# Determine the features to build based on the data columns
feature_list = {
    column: determine_features(data_all, column)
    for column in data_all.columns
}

# Encode the features, here assuming that encode_feature returns a DataFrame
encoded_features = [
    encode_feature(data_all, column, feature)
    for column, feature in feature_list
]
```

```
# Combine the encoded features into a single DataFrame
X = pd.concat(encoded_features, axis=1)

# Split data into training and evaluation sets
X_train, X_eval, y_train, y_eval = train_test_split(
    X, y, test_size=0.2, random_state=42
)

# Train a machine learning model using the features and response variable
model = xgb.XGBClassifier()
model.fit(
    X_train,
    y_train,
    early_stopping_rounds=10,
    eval_set=[(X_eval, y_eval)],
    verbose=False,
)

# Obtain SHAP values to explain the model's predictions
explainer = TreeExplainer(model)
shap_values = explainer.shap_values(X)

# Compute anomaly scores for each column based on the SHAP values
column_scores = compute_column_scores(shap_values, feature_list)
return column_scores
```

Other Applications

We've focused on how unsupervised ML can help you detect sudden structural changes in your data on an ongoing basis. However, the ML approach outlined in this chapter has two additional use cases that are worth mentioning.

The first is finding *legacy* data quality issues, which will appear as shocks and scars in the history of your data. This can be done by running the algorithm outlined in this chapter on a sequence of historical dates and investigating the anomalies you find. In fact, in Chapter 5, we'll outline how we use this process, which we call *backtesting*, to measure how effective our models are.

But beware, as this approach can come with some complications. The first is that you may find issues that are very difficult to explain. There are often changes that no one in the organization remembers, and validating whether they are concerning or not would require expensive and tedious detective work. The second complication is that you may be expecting to find some issues that simply aren't there. This often happens when known data quality issues are fixed and a team backfills the data to repair the scar. Once that happens, you should no longer be able to detect the issue in the history of your data.

The second use case is more significant, and we will touch on it only briefly here. Instead of using unsupervised ML to compare data in the same table over time, you can instead compare two samples of data from the same table (or from different tables with the same column schema) to find meaningful differences between them.

In this case, the unsupervised ML algorithm is going to detect, and help explain, any significant distribution or relationship differences between the two sets of data. Because it uses sampling, this approach can be applied to massive tables, and even to tables that reside in different source warehouses or databases!

This allows for the following kinds of applications:

- Comparing raw data from a source database to cleansed and transformed data in the destination warehouse
- Comparing the data from the current version of your ETL pipeline with the data produced by a new proposed version
- Comparing a current sample of data to a sample from the distant past
- Comparing data from different business segments, geographies, product categories, or marketing campaigns

Figure 4-8 shows how a monitoring platform can expose this feature as a custom check that users can configure and run on demand to compare and contrast datasets of interest.

Conclusion

Whether you're an experienced data scientist or new to machine learning, we hope this chapter has been a useful primer on how to build a model to detect sudden changes in the distribution of data from one day to the next. We've covered the overall concept, which relies on trying to build a classifier to predict whether a given row in the table is from today's data. If you can do this, something has clearly changed about today's data. You can use SHAP values to give individual rows in the table a score as to how much they helped the model make its determination. For the purposes of data quality monitoring, these scores can become indicators of how unusual those pieces of data are, and in what ways. This approach can even be extended to explain historical changes in your data or compare two SQL query result distributions.

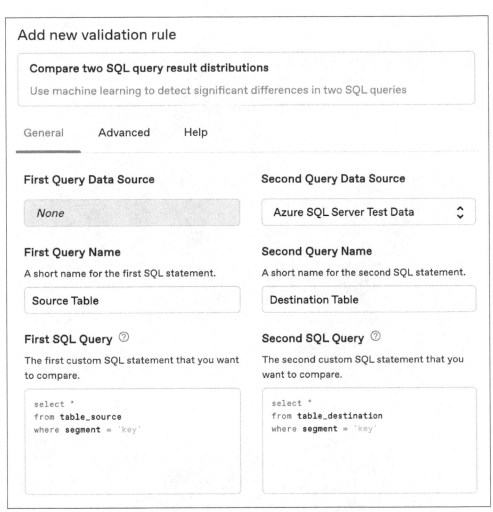

Figure 4-8. Using unsupervised ML, a data quality monitoring platform can expose a check that allows users to compare two datasets.

The steps we've just described may sound simple in practice, but everything changes when you get into the details of working with real data. Real data has seasonal trends, contains correlations that you don't want to treat as separate issues, and often gets updated in place without any indication—to name just a few hurdles. We'll discuss these challenges, and how you can overcome them, in Chapter 5.

Building a Model That Works on Real-World Data

In Chapter 4, we shared an algorithm for data quality monitoring with unsupervised machine learning. It's one thing to read about these steps, and quite another to build a model that performs well in practice on any arbitrary real-world dataset. If you don't have strategies to account for nuances like seasonality, time-based features, and correlations across columns, your model will over- or under-alert, often dramatically.

Beyond knowing the pitfalls to look out for, you'll need to continuously evaluate your model against benchmark data to figure out where and how to improve. We'll share methods for effective model testing, including thoughts on developing a library to introduce chaos into perfectly well-behaved data (cue evil laugh).

Data Challenges and Mitigations

To make your model truly valuable rather than noisy, you'll need strategies to overcome the challenges presented by data in the wild.

Seasonality

Humans are very seasonal creatures. We change our behavior patterns by hour of the day and day of the week. We pay bills on roughly the same day every month and go on holiday around the same time every year. Most data, in some way or another, is a reflection of human behavior or is affected by human behavior, and so these seasonality patterns appear in almost all data we care about.

As you'll recall from Chapter 4, our approach relies on comparing data from today to data from yesterday. But because of seasonality, it turns out this isn't actually enough. You might run into the issue that (for example) today is Monday and yesterday was

Sunday, and many of the differences in the data are due to seasonality rather than data quality.

What if, instead, you always compared today's data against data from the same day the previous week (e.g., if today is Monday, look at last week's Monday)? Unfortunately, this doesn't avoid all the potential problems. First, if your strategy only checks data from last week, you won't really know how long you've had an issue—it could have been present for the entire past week, or just appeared today. Second, what if there was a data quality issue last Monday? If today's data is normal, it might look abnormal simply because it's different from what happened last Monday. Third, what if last Monday was a holiday, so everything was just weird last Monday?

To control for these factors, it's essential to sample data *from multiple different times in the past* (yesterday, two days ago, a week ago, two weeks ago, etc.). If today's data looks "normal" when compared to any of these prior dates, then today's data must not be unusual.

Another way to combat seasonality is to generate a lot of metadata statistics automatically every time you monitor data. Then you can use time series models on that metadata over time to identify if features have a longer-term consistent seasonality trend to them and dampen those features down.

Time-Based Features

Here's a problem that you're sure to encounter almost as soon as you deploy the naive ML algorithm in the real world: there's usually at least one column in a table that is directly correlated with time, such as a timestamp or an ID. It's trivial to look at this column and know whether the data is from today or not! Before these time-correlated features soak up too much of our model's attention, we need to identify and remove them from the sample dataset entirely.

Our feature engineering for timestamps takes the delta between each timestamp and the column used to partition the data by time, so this generally removes the obvious correlations of "I have 10 different timestamps that are all correlated with time." It's the ones that are less obvious that are difficult to deal with. Examples we commonly encounter are:

- Autoincrementing IDs (each new customer gets a slightly larger ID, so you can always identify records from "today" as those having larger customer IDs)
- String- or integer-based representations of date information—such as "day of month" or "day of week"—that will always be changing
- Version identifiers for applications or logging semantics, which may change erratically or frequently depending on how often the system is updated

Some of these issues can be identified via simple summary statistics, such as checking whether a feature is always larger each day. But in practice, you'll get more robust coverage by building an additional, simple version of your model using the complete dataset. Just look for any features that are incredibly significant to this model's predictions consistently over time,[1] and take them out of the dataset for your real model.

Chaotic Tables

Datasets can be very chaotic for a few reasons. There might be humans conducting ad hoc processes (like marketing campaigns) on an unpredictable schedule that meaningfully affects the data. Alternatively, the product or service generating the data might be immature and in the process of being changed very rapidly by an Agile engineering team. If you don't account for how chaotic a table is, your model will treat all data equally and over-alert on chaotic tables while under-alerting on tables that are more stable. (We'll talk much more about alerts in Chapter 6.)

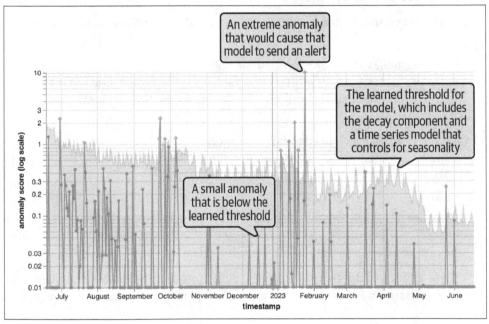

Figure 5-1. Example of table anomaly scores and learned thresholds over time.

Therefore, it's important to set thresholds for notifications by building up a time series of the severity of changes detected by the ML model. Figure 5-1 gives an example, where the overall anomaly score for the table (on a log scale) is based on

---

1 This is very important, as otherwise you could remove a data quality issue from your dataset!

the average magnitude of the SHAP values. This lets you use a time series model to learn how chaotic each table is and suggest a reasonable threshold for alerting that can move up and down dynamically over time.

To avoid noise when the model is first beginning to observe the data in the table, we recommend starting with a very conservative threshold and gradually reducing it to the level of chaos found in the dataset. You can begin with a threshold that is very, very high (such that it is almost impossible for the model to alert on the initial run) and exponentially decay that baseline threshold down toward zero; a reasonable approach is to decay by a factor of two every 10 days or so. You can then blend that base threshold with a time series model that is fit to the scores you've been logging.

Updated-in-Place Tables

In Chapter 4, we stated that our algorithm shouldn't be expected to make decisions without some notion of time. This can be surprisingly tricky in practice due to how some types of tables are updated.

You might be working with a few different types of tables in your data warehouse:

Static tables
> These are tables that don't have a time column. They can be either dimension or lookup tables (e.g., all of the demographic information known about a given entity) or summary tables (e.g., a set of summary statistics about the current state of a set of entities).
>
> For these tables, you'll need to take snapshots of the data every day, as any record could be updated at any given time (or the entire table could be dropped and replaced).

Log tables
> These are tables where the only change that ever happens is that new records are added to the existing table. No changes ever occur in old records. This is often the case with raw transactional or event-level data.
>
> These tables usually have a `created_at` time column that indicates when each record was created, and that can be used to partition the data into time-based samples.

Updated-in-place (mutating) tables
> These are tables that at first glance appear to be log tables, in that each record corresponds to a specific event or transaction, and new records are regularly being added to the table. However, the records themselves *can change after they are initially written*. For example, a table of ecommerce orders might start without a record that has the order date, but the shipping date isn't known yet—it begins as NULL and is filled in over the coming days once the shipping date is set.

These tables usually have a `created_at` time column, but they will also have an `updated_at` time column, which tracks when each record was last updated. You'll need to treat these tables carefully.

One way to detect if records in a table are frequently updated in place is to track how historical values in a metric change over time. For example, Figure 5-2 records the number of records in a table each day. The x-axis is the time column in the table (the `datecreated` column), whereas the y-axis is the date. Each day, you can compare the row count that you obtained on that day to what you had on the day prior. In Figure 5-2, squares are colored based on whether, and how much, the data has changed.

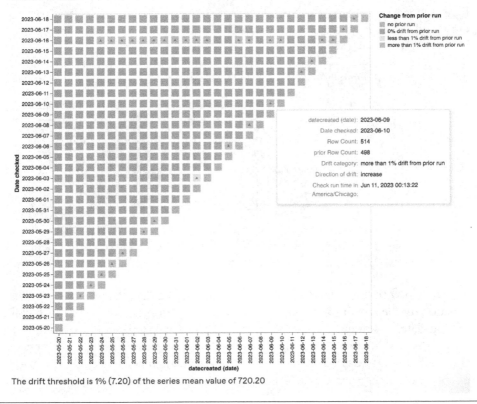

Figure 5-2. Changes in row count over time for a table. See a full-sized version of this image at https://oreil.ly/adqm_5_2.

For example, for 2023-06-09 (per `datecreated`), when we first observed records on that date, we found only 498 rows. But the second day we checked (on 2023-06-10), we found 514 rows. This indicates that more records were added on that subsequent date.

We typically observe two patterns in this visualization:

- A colored diagonal pattern means that a table has frequent updates to new data. Specifically, that new data is updated in the days immediately following its appearance in the table. The width of the diagonal indicates how long you have to wait for data to "mature" in the table. In Figure 5-2, we see a diagonal indicating that maturity takes about one day.

- A horizontal line indicates that, on a given date, a batch process was run that changed a bunch of historical data—often to address a data quality issue or otherwise migrate the dataset.

There's a third type of pattern, vertical lines of change, but this is much less common, as it would indicate there is a specific date for which data is frequently changing. For visual examples of all three patterns, see Figure 5-3.

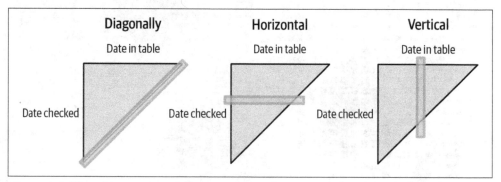

Figure 5-3. Visual patterns and their meaning when using colors to track how data changes over time in an updated-in-place table.

The problem with tables that are updated in place is that they appear to always have anomalies on the most recent date. For example, the percentage of orders with NULL shipping dates is always going to spike on recent days. However, this is really just a by-product of how data is being updated. If we compare the data from today to the data from yesterday *when we observed it yesterday*, then we would see that the percentage of NULL values in the `shipped_at` column is actually as expected.

For this reason, you should always take snapshots of the data in each table you monitor every day and compare the current data to these snapshots so that you can rule out any changes that might be due to updated-in-place dynamics. Since it can be challenging to know which tables are updated in place (and many tables will be updated in place without an `updated_at` time column), it's best to assume this is happening—and spend some extra computational resources—than risk sending repeated false positive alerts due to this issue.

Note that it can be hard to achieve a "warm start" with this approach, as you have to wait to take the snapshots of the data before you can trust that the algorithm isn't finding issues related to updated-in-place dynamics.

Column Correlations

Most datasets have a great deal of correlation structure in them (feel free to take a peek back at Figure 2-4 for an example). This can happen for several reasons. The same data may be captured in multiple different forms (e.g., identifiers and strings). Or there may be a hierarchy of identifiers that are all captured on the same table and used to group the data for different levels of business reporting. Also, tables often represent causal funnels where certain events must occur before other events can happen, and these funnels will appear as correlations in the table structure.

When columns are correlated, that means a single data quality issue could affect all those columns. If the algorithm isn't careful, it might send multiple alerts or suggest that there are many separate issues when in fact they are all related.

Data quality issues affecting multiple columns often occur in pipelines where data "fans out." For example, we might start out with a column that is an integer ID for the location of an event. Then that column is joined to a locations table with metadata like location names, dates, priority levels, etc. If the original location identifier in the log goes missing, then the join will fail, and all of the other location metadata will also go missing.

With SHAP values that credit how anomalous individual values are in the table, you can use row-level correlations to cluster the columns together and present them as a single issue to the user. For example, if one level in a hierarchy is affected by a data quality issue, we will see anomalies across multiple columns, but all for the same rows. With this insight, we can present a single anomaly rather than overwhelming users with multiple alerts about the same incident.

As an example, consider the following table, which gives some sample product data for items stocked on grocery store shelves:

Item ID	Department	Aisle	Product	Brand	Item	Size
43112	Refrigerated	Yogurt	Greek Yogurt	Chobani	0% Plain	32 oz.
43113	Refrigerated	Yogurt	Greek Yogurt	Chobani	0% Plain	64 oz.
43114	Refrigerated	Yogurt	Greek Yogurt	Chobani	2% Plain	32 oz.
43115	Refrigerated	Yogurt	Greek Yogurt	Chobani	2% Plain	64 oz.
...	...	...	...	...	...	...
43945	Refrigerated	Yogurt	Greek Yogurt	Fage	0% Plain	32 oz.
...	...	...	...	...	...	...

In a dataset like this, an anomaly might occur at the product level (all Greek Yogurt is missing), which could be caught by features derived from the Aisle column (Yogurt is anomalous), Product column (Greek Yogurt), or Brand column (a collection of specific brands are anomalous). Department is probably too highly aggregated to be sensitive to an anomaly for Greek yogurt, and the Item column is too fragmented to be easily used to detect the anomaly.

Given that our algorithm has produced the SHAP-based anomaly scores for each individual record, we can apply clustering algorithms to those anomaly scores to detect that the anomalies in these columns are all happening on the same set of rows.

Model Testing

Given all those challenges, and what is already a fairly complex algorithm, how do you ensure that the model you build actually works on real-world data? Furthermore, how do you make iterative improvements?

Collecting benchmark data where humans have labeled what's anomalous and what's not might seem reasonable at first glance, but as we've discussed elsewhere in this book, creating a human-labeled dataset where raters judge what's anomalous is extremely expensive (not to mention subjective). You'd need tens of thousands of labeled anomalies to form a robust benchmark.

So, we need a different approach. The key insight here is that realistic data quality issues are actually not that hard to *insert programmatically into datasets*. After all, issues are most often caused by code in the first place! We've found that detecting synthetic anomalies, a.k.a. "chaos," is a good proxy for detecting real data quality issues. As Patches O'Houlihan proclaims in the movie *Dodgeball*, "If you can dodge a wrench, you can dodge a ball."

Thus, the algorithm for benchmarking is roughly as follows: collect a representative sample of tabular datasets, run your model on these datasets both before and after introducing synthetic anomalies, and measure statistics around the runtimes and accuracy of your evaluation. This allows you to fine-tune your model in ways that you hope will improve your stats (e.g., by changing parameters or dampening features). Rinse and repeat.

Let's talk about what kinds of synthetic anomalies you can introduce and how, then move on to benchmarking and fine-tuning your model.

Injecting Synthetic Issues

"Chaos engineering" is the idea of purposefully creating random failures in a system to test how the system responds. One well-known example is Netflix's Chaos Monkey (*https://oreil.ly/DYkV8*), a tool that randomly terminates production instances to test a network's resiliency.

This idea translates well to testing data quality monitoring models. You can manipulate benchmark datasets with SQL to simulate real data quality problems that can occur in production systems. Since real data issues tend to affect only part of the data, it's important to also vary *how* you apply the synthetic issues: to a segment, random columns, random percentages of the data, etc. Then you can measure your model's performance according to ML metrics like sensitivity, specificity, and the area under the curve (AUC) (*https://oreil.ly/Qavzw*), and also look at other performance characteristics such as how much time the model needs and how good it is at detecting certain kinds of issues compared to others.

Example

Figure 5-4 shows a sample table of ticket sales data, each row corresponding to a listing of a number of tickets to a concert or sporting event. For example, we can see that listid number 43729 (the last row) was a listing for four tickets at $131 per ticket (a total of $524) for The Who at Reliant Stadium in Houston, Texas (seats 72k people!).

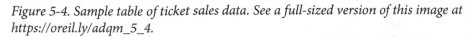

Figure 5-4. Sample table of ticket sales data. See a full-sized version of this image at https://oreil.ly/adqm_5_4.

Imagine we know that for the `numtickets` column, the maximum value is 30. One way to test whether our algorithm is capable of detecting a distributional change in the number of tickets would be to introduce some artificial chaos and change the values of the `numtickets` column to include the value 40.

It's important that we do this only for the most recent date, as we want this change to appear as a sudden anomaly in the dataset. Furthermore, to make this data quality issue a bit more subtle, we will ensure that the chaos only applies to 30% of the records. We'll include a `where_sql` clause that causes the chaos to apply only to tickets sold in `venuestate = 'NY'`.

In practice, the SQL to inject this chaos into the table looks like:

```
WITH chaosed_table AS (
    SELECT "listid",
        "listtime",
        "sellerid",
        CASE
            WHEN random() < 0.3 THEN 40
            ELSE "numtickets"
        END AS "numtickets",
        "priceperticket",
        "totalprice",
        "eventid",
        "eventname",
        "catid",
        "catgroup",
        "catname",
        "venueid",
        "venuename",
        "venuecity",
        "venuestate",
        "venueseats"
    FROM fact_listing
    WHERE listtime >= Cast(
            Cast('2022-05-04' AS DATE) AS TIMESTAMP without time zone
        )
        AND listtime < Cast(
            Cast('2022-05-05' AS DATE) AS TIMESTAMP without time zone
        )
        AND venuestate = 'NY'
),
all_other AS (
    SELECT *
    FROM    fact_listing
    WHERE   NOT (
            listtime >= cast(
                cast('2022-05-04' AS date) AS timestamp without time zone
            )
            AND listtime < cast(
                cast('2022-05-05' AS date) AS timestamp without time zone
```

```
        )
        AND     venuestate = 'NY'
    )
)
SELECT *
FROM chaos_table
UNION ALL
SELECT *
FROM all_other
```

Does this sound like a silly example? Well, you'd be surprised at how often prices can change due to a data quality error. See, for example, the slightly overpriced airline ticket in Figure 5-5.

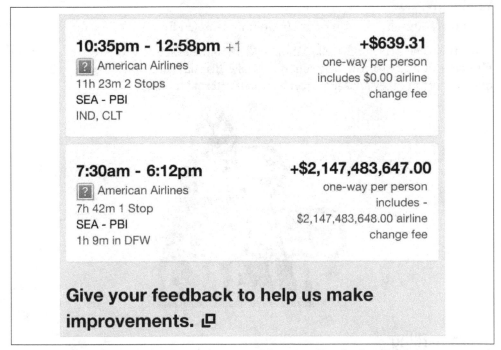

Figure 5-5. An exorbitant airline ticket price (Shaun Walker [@sbwalker], Twitter, April 2023, 4:50 p.m., https://oreil.ly/BsKtS).

If you are testing models frequently, it's helpful to encapsulate operations like these into a library. Examples of chaos operations from Anomalo's internal Chaos Llama library include:

ColumnGrow
    Multiplies a column by a random value drawn uniformly.

ColumnModeDrop

Drops rows with values equal to the mode of a given column. Requires that the mode represents at least a threshold fraction of the data, or else throws an error. This is designed to prevent chaos where the mode is very rare.

ColumnNull

Turns `table.column` into NULL for a fraction of records.

ColumnRandom

Replaces values in a column with random floats or integers within the column range, a 50/50 split of True/False for Boolean, or a hash of the string.

TableReplicate

Adds additional rows to a table (randomly sampled from the original table).

Why the Chaos Llama? Well, "Anomalo," if said sufficiently quickly, a sufficient number of times in a row, may sound a bit like "llama." And so we chose the llama as our mascot, and they appear frequently in our internal tooling.

Benchmarking

Benchmarks are composed of many sample datasets; we call these *backtests*. Each backtest represents a historical sample from a dataset over a consecutive period of days. For each backtest, you can run your model on each day in sequential order. This simulates the dataset being configured and new records arriving each day. At this stage, important data points to capture are an overall anomaly score for each table (the same type of score used in Figure 5-1) and the learned dynamic threshold for alerting. This will give you a baseline of how anomalous your model believes the benchmark data is *before* any synthetic anomalies are introduced.

Once your initial run is complete, you can then cycle back through the data—only this time, each day you'll introduce a random chaos operation into the data. Then, you can rerun your model to see if it's able to detect the chaos. Again, keeping track of the anomaly score will tell you how sensitive your model is to each particular chaos operation.

For example, Figure 5-6 summarizes the results for the backtest on a single table containing data from April 29 to May 28. We begin on April 29, build our model for that date, log all of the results, and then step through each date in turn until we finish on May 28. Then we repeat this process while injecting synthetic data quality issues into the dataset.

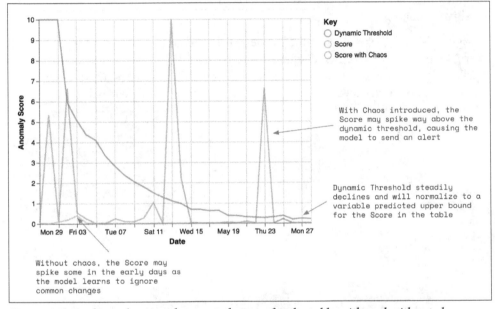

Figure 5-6. Backtest showing the anomaly score for the table with and without chaos. The model learns a threshold for alerting as it experiences more and more anomalies over time.

The yellow line shows the anomaly score from the model before any chaos is introduced. You can see that it rises on May 3 but otherwise remains close to zero. It's common for a table to have higher anomaly scores in the early days, as the model is still learning what columns and features represent intermittent changes that need to be dampened to find true anomalies. The fact that the score stays near zero indicates that, once these are controlled for, the dataset is very predictable and regular.

The blue line shows the threshold for the anomaly score. This begins at 10, the highest possible anomaly score (representing an extreme change that affects 100% of the data). We hold the score at this highest value for three days, and then it begins to exponentially decay. At the end of the 30 days, the threshold has fallen all the way to below 0.3, which would be sensitive enough to detect a moderate anomaly.

Finally, the red line shows what happens to the anomaly score when chaos is added to the dataset. On the second day, the score jumps over 5—an extreme anomaly likely caused by a significant chaos operation. But the threshold is still so high (10) that this issue would be suppressed. We want to be conservative about alerting, especially in the early days.

By the fourth day, however, the score jumps above 6.5, and this is just high enough to pass the threshold. Even in the first week, a sufficiently anomalous change in the data can cause the model to alert. As we go past day 30, and ultimately day 90, the model becomes well calibrated to the level of expected noise in the data and is much more sensitive to chaos.

In Figure 5-7, the y-axis shows nine backtests for nine sample datasets, each evaluated over 30 days (the x-axis). A red square indicates that the model sends an alert, while a yellow square indicates that it was close to alerting. Gray squares are days when the model does not alert. As you can see, alerts are infrequent in the early days.

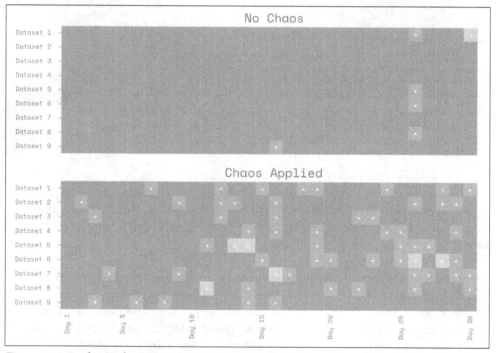

Figure 5-7. Backtests for nine sample datasets over 30 days. See a full-sized version of this image at https://oreil.ly/adqm_5_7.

Comparing the top and bottom panels, it's clear that the model is quite sensitive to the introduction of chaos, and that this is true for each of the different datasets. However, in the bottom panel, there are many days that are still gray (no alert)—even though we are applying a chaos operation every day. This can happen for a few different reasons:

- The threshold is still set very high, as we gradually decay the threshold from 10 (very hard to alert) down towards the learned threshold for the dataset. Even by day 30, this decay is not yet complete.
- In some cases, we introduced chaos that is very rare. It may be targeted at only 1% of records, making the anomaly much harder to detect.
- In some cases, the chaos that we introduce may not actually change the data. For instance, if we change 5% of the values in a column to be NULL, this won't make a difference if 99% of the values in the column were already NULL.

Analyzing performance

To understand how well the model performs, there are different types of statistics you can compute for the entire benchmark, such as AUC, F1 score, precision, and recall.

No matter what metrics you choose to look at, there are many different ways of slicing and dicing the results:

- By dataset
- By how many days the model has been running
- By the type of chaos used
- By the percentage of records the chaos is applied to (the *chaos fraction*)

In practice, we look at all of these, and more, to better understand how the model is performing and how we might improve it.

The chaos fraction is particularly useful, as it gives you a sense of:

- How well the model is performing at the limit—when applying chaos to the entire dataset, you expect the model to perform very, very well.
- Where the model begins to be unable to detect issues given the sample size of data that you are working with.

In Figure 5-8, the x-axis is the fraction of records that we've applied a given chaos operation to (ranging from 1% to 95% of records), and the y-axis represents a performance statistic.

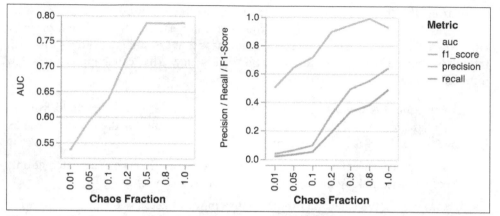

Figure 5-8. Performance metrics for a model benchmark over different chaos fractions.

The first panel plots the AUC statistic. This compares the anomaly score that we produce for a given date (our "prediction") to the binary "outcome" of whether chaos was introduced on that date. The AUC measures the area under a curve traced out by varying a decision threshold for the score from 0.0 up to 10.0 and measuring the false positive and true positive rates for classifying each {table, date} combination as either having chaos (an anomaly) or not. When the AUC is near 0.50, the model is performing no better than a random guess. When the AUC is near 1.0, the model is perfectly able to detect chaos in the data.

We see that the AUC steadily rises from near 0.50 at 1% chaos, to close to 0.80 at 50% chaos and above. In practice, these AUC statistics underrepresent how well the model performs for several reasons:

- Some of the {table, date} combinations that do not have chaos will actually have real anomalies in the source data that we would want to alert on. In other words, not all of the "negative" examples here are true negatives.

- Some of our chaos operations are affecting a much smaller percentage of records than the chaos fraction would suggest. The fraction places a maximum on the percentage of records affected—if we're altering the mode of a column, or an infrequent value, or making a change that already exists in the data, the chaos may be impossible to detect.

- We're measuring performance over the first 30 days of the model run, but in practice, we see the performance of the model continue to increase dramatically up to 90 days.

While the AUC is helpful to understand how good our model is at distinguishing if chaos was applied, it doesn't explain if the model is doing a good job of setting a threshold. The second panel directly measures precision, recall, and F1 score based on the decision to alert if the score is above or below the learned threshold.

In this context, precision measures what fraction of the time the model alerts when there is a chaos operation present. This can help you understand how often you might have false positive alerts. As you can see in Figure 5-8, when the chaos affects a very small percentage of records, precision is about 50%. But when the chaos affects a large percentage of records, it's up to 90%.

Recall measures the percentage of chaos operations the model is able to alert on. Returning to Figure 5-8, you can see that it begins quite low (near 0) but rises to almost 50% when chaos is applied to more than half of the data. Again, recall may be low because chaos operations are difficult to detect, due to the reasons stated above.

One way to improve recall is to make adjustments to the algorithm for thresholding (start lower, decay faster, or converge to a lower quantile estimate for the score), thus making the model more sensitive to chaos. However, this increases the likelihood of false positives (and alert fatigue), especially in the early days when the model is still being calibrated.

The F1 score takes into account both the precision and the recall and is computed as `2*((precision*recall)/(precision+recall))`. There are many changes that might improve precision but not recall, or vice versa, and the F1 score gives an indication of whether a change is good or bad based on the combined effect. Note that in practice, the cost of false positives and false negatives can be estimated directly and used to make decisions about how to improve and calibrate the model.

Putting it together with pseudocode

The following Python pseudocode gives an example of how you could apply the approach we've just outlined to benchmark your algorithm. It assumes you have the `detect_anomalies` method from Chapter 4, and a collection of tables and their configuration information. It then runs a backtest for each table with and without chaos and summarizes the anomaly scores for each. Then it computes the AUC of the algorithm based on how accurate it is at "predicting" which results had chaos introduced.

Please don't take this code too literally, as it's just meant to illustrate the concepts and how they fit together at a high level. In particular, we've glossed over the fact that the algorithm may maintain state from one run to the next (e.g., the threshold calculation), and we haven't produced any details for the random chaos generation.

We start by defining how to calculate anomaly scores for a given date range and table:

```python
# General imports
import datetime as dt
from sklearn.metrics import roc_auc_score

# Import hypothetical sub-modules that perform more detailed tasks
from chaos import generate_random_chaos
from prior_chapter import detect_anomalies

def calculate_anomaly_scores(
    table: str,
    time_column: str,
    current_date: dt.date,
    prior_date: dt.date,
    sample_size: int = 10_000
) -> float:
    column_scores = detect_anomalies(
        table, time_column, current_date, prior_date, sample_size
    )
    return sum(column_scores.values())
```

Then we backtest the anomaly detection logic over a range of dates to get the anomaly scores with and without chaos:

```python
def backtest(
    table: str,
    time_column: str,
    start_date: dt.date,
    number_of_days: int
) -> list[list[float]]:
    anomaly_scores = []
    chaos_anomaly_scores = []

    for day in range(number_of_days):
        current_date = start_date + dt.timedelta(days=day)
        prior_date = current_date - dt.timedelta(days=1)

        overall_score = calculate_anomaly_scores(
            table, time_column, current_date, prior_date
        )
        anomaly_scores.append(overall_score)

        # Introduce chaos and recalculate
        table_chaos = generate_random_chaos(table, time_column, current_date)
        chaos_overall_score = calculate_anomaly_scores(
            table_chaos, time_column, current_date, prior_date
        )
        chaos_anomaly_scores.append(chaos_overall_score)

    return anomaly_scores, chaos_anomaly_scores
```

Next, we run backtests on multiple table configurations to benchmark their performance:

```
def benchmark(
    table_configurations: list[dict],
    number_of_days: int
) -> list[dict]:
    """
    Runs backtests on multiple table configurations to benchmark their performance.
    """
    benchmark_results = []

    for config in table_configurations:
        anomaly_scores, chaos_anomaly_scores = backtest(
            config['table'],
            config['time_column'],
            config['start_date'],
            number_of_days
        )
        benchmark_results.append({
            'table': config['table'],
            'anomaly_scores': anomaly_scores,
            'chaos_anomaly_scores': chaos_anomaly_scores
        })

    return benchmark_results
```

Finally, we calculate a single AUC metric (as an example model metric) based on the anomaly and chaos scores from all the tables:

```
def calculate_global_auc(benchmark_results: list[dict]) -> float:
    """
    Calculate a single AUC based on the anomaly and chaos scores from all tables.
    """
    all_anomaly_scores = []
    all_chaos_anomaly_scores = []

    for result in benchmark_results:
        all_anomaly_scores.extend(result['anomaly_scores'])
        all_chaos_anomaly_scores.extend(result['chaos_anomaly_scores'])

    # Create labels: 0 for anomaly, 1 for chaos
    y_true = [0] * len(all_anomaly_scores) + [1] * len(all_chaos_anomaly_scores)

    # Concatenate scores
    y_scores = all_anomaly_scores + all_chaos_anomaly_scores

    # Calculate AUC
    auc = roc_auc_score(y_true, y_scores)

    return auc
```

Improving the Model

Benchmarking and analyzing performance statistics is extraordinarily helpful to understand and debug your model. It's also a way to prove to users that your system is working as expected.

But one of the most important ways you can use this data is to validate changes to your model, to ensure you're fine-tuning it in a way that will add value. Figure 5-9 shows an example of summary statistics computed for a benchmark, with the goal of measuring if a change to the model is moving the stats in the right direction.

Statistic	Definition	Baseline	New	% Change	Implication
Hours	The number of hours to run the benchmark in a massively parallel environment	2.6	3.1	16%	This change is increasing the compute costs, and we may want to optimize it further
Alert %	How often the model will alert without chaos being introduced	1.92%	2.02%	5%	We are slightly more likely to alert (we are finding more anomalies in the data without chaos)
Precision	Fraction of time that alerts occur when chaos was introduced	0.858	0.866	1%	False positives are improved
Recall	Fraction of time that we alert when chaos was introduced	0.117	0.132	11%	False negatives are improved
F1-Score	A form of average (harmonic mean) of the precision and recall	0.205	0.228	10%	Both false positives and false negatives improve
Mean Score	The mean score when chaos has not been introduced	0.132	0.150	12%	The score is 12% higher even without chaos
AUC	Area under the curve for the scores when used to predict if there was chaos or not	0.617	0.624	1%	The overall AUC is slightly higher
AUC - 0.5	Improvement in the AUC above a random model	0.117	0.124	5%	The anomaly scores are now a better predictor of whether chaos is introduced, indepenent of our thresholding strategy

Figure 5-9. Summary statistics and implications for a model benchmark. See a full-sized version of this image at https://oreil.ly/adqm_5_9.

The hypothetical update being evaluated in Figure 5-9 was a new type of feature that allowed the model to be even more sensitive to changes in patterns in string columns (think phone numbers, identifiers, etc.). The change increased the benchmark's runtime meaningfully, which suggests it may be important to optimize the change further to avoid increasing the overall latency and costs of the model.

However, on the positive side, the change significantly improved both precision and recall by reducing the number of false negatives. The AUC also improved, although the percentage improvement appears small on an absolute basis. But if instead we ask how much greater than 0.5 did the AUC rise (since that indicates random behavior), the AUC improvement is actually $(0.624 - 0.5) / (0.617 - 0.5) - 1 = 5\%$ better, which is significant.

Conclusion

We've explored some of the attributes of real-world data that are likely to require care when building your model—such as the fact that data is correlated or gets updated in place. And we've walked through how you can benchmark your models by injecting chaos into sample datasets. The outcome of this testing will help you measure your model's performance and iterate on it over time.

It isn't easy to build a model that alerts appropriately for real-world data issues—not missing important issues, nor over-alerting on minor changes. Once you have a high-quality model, though, what really matters is how you use it to empower the humans responsible for data quality. In the next chapter, we'll explain how to leverage your model's output to build effective notifications that help users get to the bottom of unusual changes in their data.

## CHAPTER 6

Implementing Notifications While Avoiding Alert Fatigue

What good would a monitoring system be if it didn't alert you when something went wrong? Yet alerts are both the essence and the Achilles' heel of monitoring. Done right, notifications will reach the correct people via the appropriate channels, help them understand the severity of the issue, and even point them to the root cause for fast resolution. Done wrong, notifications will spam too many people, lack context, and be difficult to act on. They'll be untrustworthy—and ultimately ignored.

Alert fatigue is one of the greatest reasons that data quality monitoring efforts fail, especially as enterprises scale (see the sidebar "Alert Fatigue" on page 20). If you have dozens of people involved in data quality and thousands of tables triggering alerts, that's a lot of employee time and energy being wasted if those alerts are unhelpful, confusing, or noisy.

In this chapter, we'll share a variety of techniques you can use to ensure your notifications are empowering your team to fix data quality issues. We'll cover the steps in the issue resolution process and how notifications can be designed to help at each stage, even with root cause analysis. We'll talk about how you find the right audience for any given notification and the right delivery mechanism. And we'll explore many strategies for avoiding alert fatigue so that your system respects what may be our most valuable human resource: our attention.

How Notifications Facilitate Data Issue Response

You can monitor data quality as much as you want—you'll only actually improve data quality if your monitoring results in productive actions. Notifications are the crucial link between your monitoring system and the results it's trying to achieve.

They make it possible for a human to take the steps that lead to a true understanding and resolution of a data quality issue.

Regardless of the details of the notification itself, which we'll get to later, the response usually follows the same steps. These steps are good to have in mind as we discuss the requirements for building good notifications. A quality notification will empower humans at every stage in the response process.

Triage

The triage step can be summed up as "deciding if the issue is concerning or not." For example, a concerning alert for an ecommerce business might be a large drop in the number of checkout conversion events tracked on Android devices. On the other hand, a decrease in the number of checkout conversion events across the board on a holiday might not be so concerning to the business—unless it's Black Friday.

For a bank that gets credit card data from a third party to use in a fraud model, a high-priority issue might be a sudden increase in the number of NULL values for a column that tracks recent transactions. A sudden increase in NULLs can be especially catastrophic for models (see the section "NULL increases" on page 52), and this is an issue the business will want to follow up on quickly. Conversely, they might not be as concerned if they see a change in the distribution of credit scores after launching a product targeted at a new customer segment.

Recall that automated data quality monitors are looking for significant, unexpected changes in the data values—they are agnostic about whether these changes *actually matter* to the business. So, in this chapter, we'll spend a lot of time talking about how you can make notifications easier to triage and, in many cases, even mute some kinds of notifications so that your team doesn't spend a lot of time looking at low-priority alerts.

Routing

Once you've determined the severity of an issue, the next step is to decide who should be notified so that further investigation or resolution can be undertaken. This process depends greatly on how your data organization is structured. Table 6-1 shows a few examples of different functional teams and how they might be involved in following up on different kinds of issues.

Table 6-1. Example data quality issues mapped to teams

Problem	Responsible team
A service that is responsible for some activity in the app is failing intermittently, causing missing data.	Engineering infrastructure
A code change was made that caused an application to log duplicate events in certain circumstances.	Product engineering
A third-party provider has changed their API and did not communicate about that change.	Data partnerships
A configuration change was made to how advertising campaigns were run that removed tracking information.	Marketing operations
An ETL process that previously ran every hour is now scheduled to run only every six hours.	Data engineering
A transformation that uses a CASE WHEN SQL clause to remap categories was changed, and some categories were dropped, resulting in NULL values.	Analytics engineering

Routing can be quite complex. You'll most likely have different audiences for data quality issues depending on the domain; for instance, a separate team for data about ad campaigns versus data about customers. At times, you may need to involve multiple teams to provide all the necessary context. Later in the chapter, we'll talk about how you can make sure notifications get to the right people while avoiding the mistake of creating too broad of an audience.

Resolution

This is the actual work required to fix the data quality issue (the shock) and/or back-fill historical data (the scar). It's often tracked in a separate system like Linear, GitHub Issues, or Jira. The resolution process depends highly on how a data quality issue was introduced and what, if any, control the organization has over the production, transmission, or transformation of the data. We aren't going to spend too much time on the nuts and bolts of resolution in this book, but we will talk later on about how root cause analysis can aid issue resolution.

Documentation

Finally, when closing out an issue, it's essential to document what (if any) actions were taken to fix the issue. Many issues recur with some small variations, and having a history of how issues were handled in the past can be a great information repository for future issues that may be similar. Furthermore, fixing data quality issues is far from straightforward, and in some cases, mistakes are made—the logic behind the fix might not be sound or might result in unintended side effects. Without documentation, it can be difficult to go back and reverse or otherwise remedy a bad fix.

Taking Action Without Notifications

Before going further, we should acknowledge that notifications don't have to be the only trigger for taking action to resolve a data quality issue. Let's explore the limited scenarios where you can take action without a notification.

Some teams integrate data quality monitors directly into their orchestration tools and flows (e.g., Airflow, dbt). Every time the data is loaded into a staging environment, they run a suite of data quality checks. If the checks pass, the data is copied into a production environment and "published" for downstream use cases. If the checks fail, rather than notifying someone, automated scripts might clean up some data quality issues, such as duplicate records. You can imagine a rule that says to retain only the most recent customer record according to a timestamp, for example.

These kinds of automated tests can be valuable in certain scenarios. For instance, they may stop the data from being published, and in some cases, late or no data is better than wrong data (when using it to make irreversible decisions, for example). Or the "fixes" that are applied may be tantamount to "retries." Especially for data freshness or volume issues, sometimes if you wait for a bit, the issue resolves itself. In complex distributed orchestrations, it can be difficult to ensure everything is scheduled appropriately, and so having retries built into the system can make it more robust.

But when the underlying data quality issue is truly just bad data, then papering over the issue with a fix that mutates the data is generally a bad idea. While it can ensure that downstream systems work as expected (the data loads into a typed field; no exceptions are thrown downstream), it's really just burying the issue and preventing anyone from realizing that it is there. It is also introducing bias into the data that may affect decisions or ML models in unexpected ways.

There are a few other scenarios where you may not need to set up notifications because you are examining the system's output directly. For instance, you might use an API to interact with your data quality monitoring system, so you take complete control of its responses. This may be useful if you're performing a data migration and want to run checks and retrieve their status from the command line. Or you might run checks to generate dashboards that you intend to review by hand on each scheduled run. However, situations like these are by definition manual and don't scale.

With that out of the way, let's go back to notifications, the primary vehicle by which monitoring results in actions that improve data quality, and the focus of this chapter.

Anatomy of a Notification

Given the steps that need to be taken in the resolution process, the question we have to ask when designing a data quality monitoring system is: How do we create notifications that facilitate these steps as much as possible, making issues easy to triage, route, resolve, and document?

Let's begin by defining, at a high level, the key components that should be part of the notification itself—its anatomy. Next, we'll move on to all the decisions you need to make outside of the contents of the notification, such as how you deliver notifications, avoid alert fatigue, and provide additional context for root cause analysis.

For this anatomy lesson, Figure 6-1 provides a sample Slack notification that we'll dissect together.

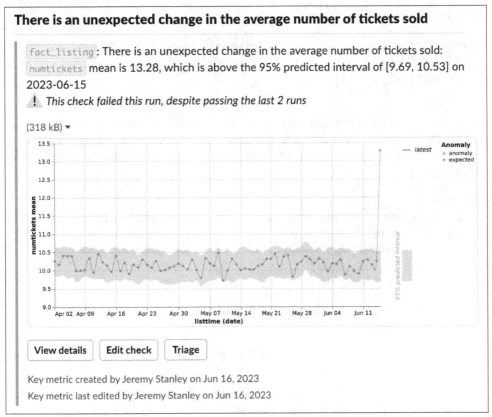

Figure 6-1. Sample Slack notification for a data quality issue. See a full-sized version of this image at https://oreil.ly/adqm_6_1.

Visualization

As Jill Hardy pointed out (*https://oreil.ly/ejHOM*), a visualization is worth a thousand data points.[1] A graphic can contain a ton of information about the underlying issue, how severe it is, and what (if any) next steps may be required.

We include one, and only one, visualization in every notification, and the type of visualization varies with the check and issue found. More details can always be found by clicking on "View details" and going to the full report.

It's important that the visualization shows the current issue but also provides some context or history. There may be many users who will see notifications but who may not be active participants in the monitoring platform. Keep in mind that if the visualization is too complex, though, users won't be able to quickly understand it.

Actions

It's important to make notifications immediately actionable. We recommend supporting three different actions right from the notification (you can see these actions as buttons at the bottom of Figure 6-1):

View details
> Allows the user to investigate the issue and understand more of the context and history behind it. This action takes users right into the data quality monitoring platform, where they can see additional visualizations, samples of records, summaries of actions taken, etc.

Edit check
> Brings up the edit configuration for the check that sent this notification. This makes it easy for the user to go in and change the configuration so that the check is better targeted to an issue they care about or is less likely to send notifications in the future.

Triage
> Brings the user directly into a triage flow on the platform, where they can do one of the following:
>
> - Acknowledge: alert others that they have acknowledged the issue and are investigating further.
>
> - Resolve: resolve the issue, either because it has been fixed or because it is not important to address or was expected.
>
> - File a ticket: create a ticket for additional work, which they can either undertake directly in the platform via API or track in a ticketing system like Jira.

---

1 Jill Hardy, "Why a Visualization Is Worth a Thousand Data Points," *Looker* (blog), July 18, 2019.

For example, an engineer may need to change how events are being logged to fix this underlying issue. See Figure 6-2 for a screenshot of triage options.

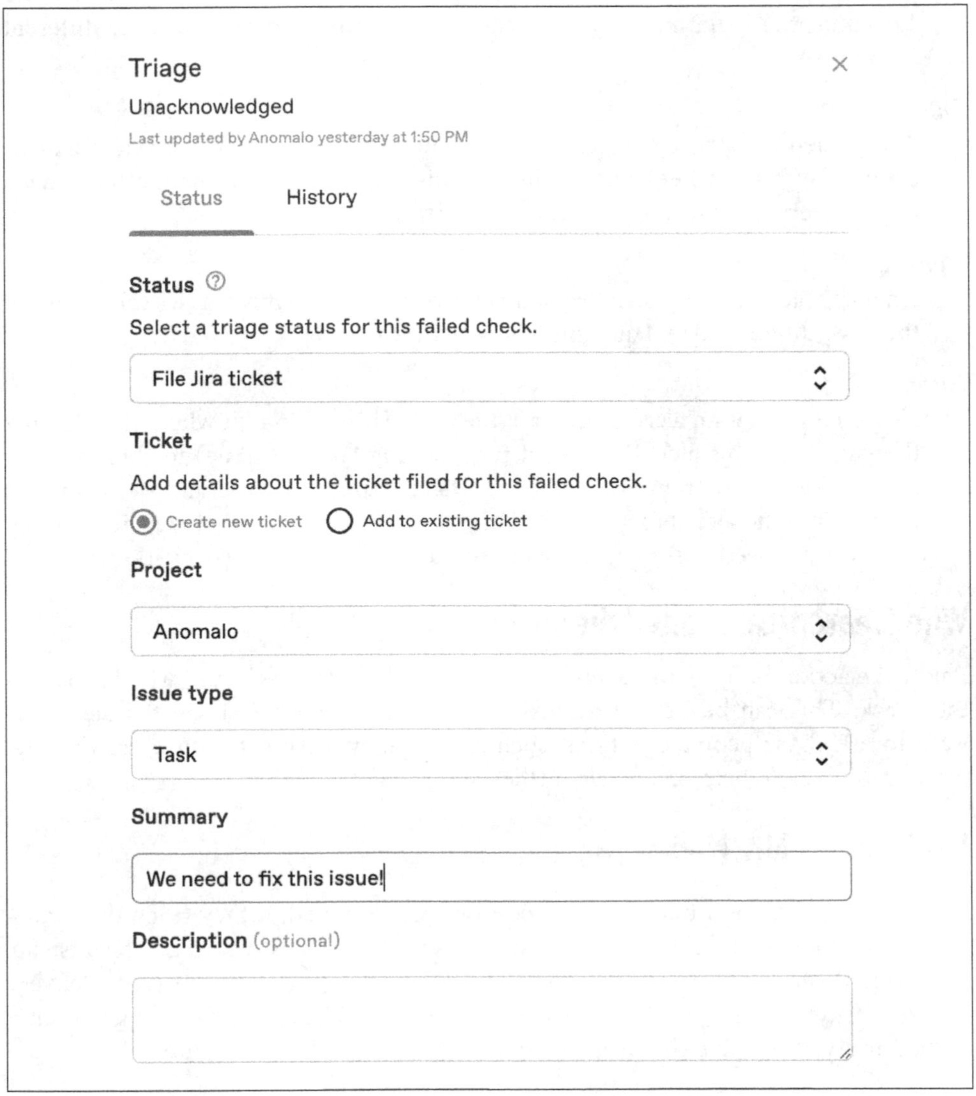

Triage

Unacknowledged

Last updated by Anomalo yesterday at 1:50 PM

Status   History

Status ⑦

Select a triage status for this failed check.

File Jira ticket

Ticket

Add details about the ticket filed for this failed check.

◉ Create new ticket   ○ Add to existing ticket

Project

Anomalo

Issue type

Task

Summary

We need to fix this issue!

Description (optional)

Figure 6-2. Example triage options.

Text Description

In addition to a visualization, some text information can be helpful to give more context about the issue that was detected. We generally recommend three different text components:

Title
> A user-defined string that represents the intent or purpose of the check, often supplied by users when creating checks. This helps pass additional business, data, or engineering context to whomever ultimately receives the alert.

Summary
> An automatically generated text summary of the alert that identifies the nature of the issue discovered and quantifies how significant it is.

History
> How many times an alert has fired in the past. This helps a lot when investigating the issue. Has this alert been silent (i.e., passing without issue) for hundreds of days? Yikes—something dramatic must have happened! In contrast, is this the fourth time the alert has gone off in a row? That could mean there's an ongoing issue we still need to fix, or we might need to reconfigure the check itself.

Who Created/Last Edited the Check

Below the action buttons we identify who first created the check, and who last edited the check. This can be helpful context because whoever is receiving the alert may want to ask those people questions, such as why they set up this check in the first place or who could help investigate further or resolve the issue.

Delivering Notifications

No matter how thoughtfully your notifications are designed, if they reach the wrong people or go into an inbox that no one is checking, they won't get results. So, it's essential that your monitoring platform integrates with many different delivery channels and lets users configure how notifications are delivered. You can get a sense of the variety of possible channels by looking at the dropdown in Figure 6-3.

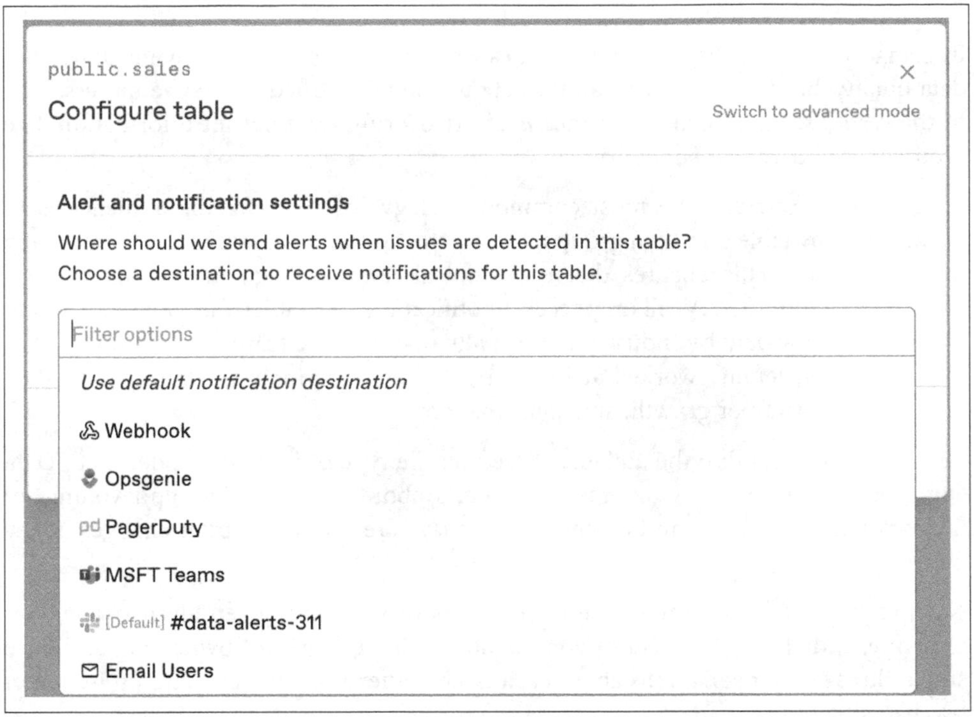

Figure 6-3. Example alert and notification destinations.

There are really three dimensions to this notification delivery: (1) *who* gets the notification, (2) *how* they get it (In their email inbox? Slack? Do they get paged?), and (3) *when* they get it (immediately or in a summary?).

Notification Audience

Who should get notified is a key decision and essential for reducing alert fatigue. A large company may have hundreds of individuals interested in seeing alerts about a very wide array of data quality issues. If everyone received every alert, it would be completely overwhelming!

When thinking about your audience, focus on ownership and context. Notifications only create value if action is taken. So, whoever is receiving the notifications should have *a high degree of ownership* over data quality for the associated tables. They must be incentivized to own the notifications and their triage and routing. You also need to ensure that you've included people who will bring in the necessary *context*. In some cases, there might be multiple people required to understand the issue and decide what next steps should be taken.

Assuming you've controlled for ownership and sufficient context, you then want to minimize the audience that is exposed to notifications. Notifications are distracting:

each human that sees them has to stop what they are otherwise doing and process the information. You might have many parties who are interested in following along with data quality, but that doesn't mean they should all be notified. If they're not essential to the response, give them other means of discovering the relevant information, like reports, dashboards, or summaries.

To get more concrete, the most common strategy for defining the audience is to group alerts by table and then group tables by the domain of users who are interested in those tables. This ensures that each topical domain (e.g., marketing, finance, growth, operations, etc.) will only receive notifications for tables that they care about. Domains vary widely by industry and usually map to how teams are organized. For example, when Jeremy worked at Instacart, the domains included logistics, catalog, advertising, consumer growth, and consumer app.

You can also determine the audience based on the *type* of issue being detected. Data engineering may be most interested in alerts about the freshness and volume of tables, whereas analytics and business users may care the most about changes in key metrics.

No matter what, an essential rule of thumb is to send any given alert to one, and only one, audience. This ensures you maintain a high degree of ownership and have single-threaded conversations about each issue. Otherwise, you can end up in one of two bad situations:

Low ownership
  Multiple audiences get each alert, and individuals in each group assume that the other group is looking at the alert.

Duplicate efforts
  Multiple audiences get an alert, and there are now two separate conversations and work streams on triage and resolution of the underlying issue.

Notification Channels

Different audiences will have different preferences for how to receive notifications. And some types of notifications are better suited for an email versus an urgent ping. Here are the primary channels that you'll want your data quality monitoring system to integrate with, and how they tend to get used at most businesses.

Email

Email, the most common form of asynchronous communication, is often used to send summary notifications (e.g., a weekly list of issues and statuses) that aren't intended to be responded to quickly. However, in some organizations, email is still the dominant form of communication, so email alerts can be the primary channel.

Real-time communication

Today, most teams want to receive notifications via a real-time communications provider, like Slack or Microsoft Teams. Commonly, teams will want to set up one or more groups (such as Slack channels) where the relevant audience(s) receive their data quality notifications.

Real-time communication affords some time-saving tactics that wouldn't be as easy to achieve by other means. For example, on Slack, many teams use emoji reactions to help quickly triage and manage notification status, as shown in Figure 6-4. From the notification itself, it's also easy to start a conversation thread to track investigation/triage or resolution while maintaining shared context.

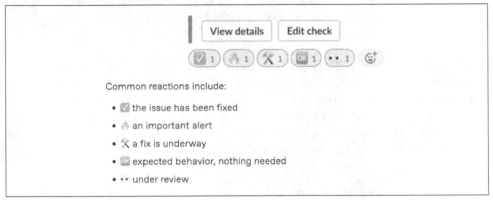

Figure 6-4. Example of common emoji reactions to alerts in Slack or Microsoft Teams.

PagerDuty or Opsgenie-type platforms (alerting, on-call management)

For the most important checks (these should be rare), you may want to "wake up" someone who is designated to respond to the issue with an alerting or on-call system such as PagerDuty or Opsgenie.

Ticketing platforms (Jira, ServiceNow)

In rare cases, you may even want to create a work item for someone any time a check fails by plugging your notifications directly into a ticketing platform. However, we recommend having a human in the middle to evaluate and triage the issue before creating the work ticket. Otherwise, you may end up with tickets that are not actionable or important.

Webhooks

A webhook is a general-purpose means of programmatically notifying another arbitrary system over the web. By supporting webhooks, you ensure that users can route notifications into arbitrary systems that don't fit into the previous categories. For example, some companies may have enterprise notification routing systems they have purchased or built internally, and they'd like to send alerts to these systems and then apply additional business logic or rules on how those notifications are delivered to end users.

Notification Timing

In general, there are two strategies for *when* to send notifications:

- Send notifications for failures as soon as the check completes (in real time), so the notification channel becomes a "log" of the failures as they are computed.
- Wait for all checks for a specific set of data (a table, schema, or other grouping) to complete, and then send a single notification with a summary of all passing and/or failing checks.

We strongly recommend the first approach for a few reasons. First, it allows users to receive notifications as soon as an issue is identified, leading to faster response times. Especially when checks are being applied to large datasets and/or are leveraging machine learning, the run times for different checks can vary dramatically. If you wait for all checks to complete to send a single summary notification, you may delay the arrival of some notifications by many hours, exacerbating the harm of a data quality issue.

A second point is that, typically, summary notifications are sent even if there's no data quality issue. These "all green" alerts can be comforting, but they require the user to consume something that requires no action—which can inadvertently drive alert fatigue. Will people still pay attention when a summary arrives containing important failures?

Finally, a given set of data might have multiple data quality issues. We've seen value in having each notification arrive separately, so conversations about different issues can happen underneath the corresponding data quality notification. With a summary alert, a confusing thread can result as users discuss or triage multiple unrelated issues.

Avoiding Alert Fatigue

How to avoid overwhelming your users with noisy notifications is one of the trickiest problems when setting up a data quality monitoring system. To some degree, all the advice in this chapter so far has been designed to mitigate the risk of alert fatigue—from narrowing your audience for notifications, to including UX elements that help with quick triage. In this section, though, we'll explore more direct techniques to limit the number of low-value alerts your team receives.

Scheduling Checks in the Right Order

How checks are scheduled is one of the biggest sources of false-positive notifications in many monitoring systems. That's because there are two naive approaches to scheduling your data quality checks, and both are problematic.

The first approach is to automatically run all your checks each time you finish processing a new set of incoming data. For example, at the end of your Airflow directed acyclic graph (DAG) for updating a table, you might programmatically trigger data quality checks via API for the newest date that is loaded into the table. The second naive approach is to run checks every day on a set schedule. For instance, you might expect some third-party data to arrive each day by 5 a.m. ET, so you run all of your data quality checks at 7 a.m. ET.

The problem with both these approaches is that you will often end up running checks on incomplete data. If you're running checks on a set schedule and the data is delayed, then all of the checks may fail or throw exceptions because there is no data. And in either scenario, the data might not be fully delivered when you run the checks, meaning that validation rules that are comparing across tables or aggregating data will almost certainly fail. Any metrics you're monitoring will look anomalous, too. Incomplete data is almost always biased—by time of day, the subset that was available or loaded, or simply the obvious: total volume.

So, how do you avoid running checks on data that hasn't even fully arrived and creating a bunch of noisy alerts? The best approach is to first set up checks to see if you have sufficient *freshness* and *volume* within a specific partition of the data (often a day or an hour of data as specified in a partitioned time column). Then, only run your deep data quality checks after those checks pass.

One way to solve this with a data quality monitoring platform is as follows (see Figure 6-5). As part of the system behavior, set up a "data freshness" check that looks for records within each date partition. Since not all data is delivered at the same cadence, this check should learn and adapt to variations, like if data typically doesn't arrive on certain days of the week. Once "data freshness" completes, run a "data volume" check, which ensures that the volume of records is within the expected predicted distribution of record counts for that specific time period (using a time series model that controls for seasonality, trend, variance changes, etc.). Only once data freshness and data volume have run should you kick off the deep data quality checks on that new partition of data.

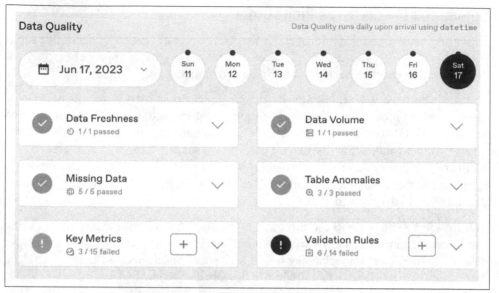

Figure 6-5. Scheduling data checks in the right order. Data Freshness and Data Volume checks run every 15 minutes, and "gate" the deep data quality checks shown below. All of the other checks (Missing Data, Table Anomalies, etc.) only run when we are certain they won't trigger false positive notifications due to freshness or data volume issues.

Clustering Alerts Using Machine Learning

Another source of alert fatigue is when your system fires duplicate alerts that spring from the same issue. There are several reasons this can happen. First, data freshness and volume issues can "cascade" downstream into derived tables that depend on the upstream table. Second, there can be multiple columns in a table that are all tightly related to one another and may all reflect the same underlying data quality issue. Finally, exogenous effects—that may appear as data quality issues but really are changes in the product behavior, or the world the product is interacting with—can cause a wide variety of related effects in multiple columns or tables.

This means that clustering or deduping alerts is an important feature of a monitoring system. When duplicate alerts happen within the same table, you can use machine learning to cluster them. Assuming your data quality issue can be mapped down to individual records, you can classify each record as being either "good" or "bad" in the context of the issue. You can then compute how correlated the "bad" and "good" records are across multiple data quality issues and determine if they are likely identifying the same set of bad records. As explained in Chapter 4, machine learning algorithms that can allocate credit for the anomalies they detect down to individual values can similarly cluster issues together.

Some teams will use data lineage to cluster data quality issues across multiple tables. Figure 6-6 shows a screenshot of lineage. When a table is failing freshness or volume, you can look upstream to see if tables that feed into this table are also failing and cluster alerts in that manner.

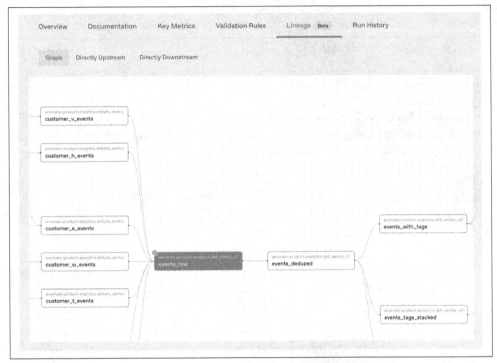

Figure 6-6. Lineage showing how issues can affect upstream and downstream tables. See a full-sized version of this image at https://oreil.ly/adqm_6_6.

Suppressing Notifications

A large part of managing alert fatigue is suppressing notifications before they even reach users. Let's explore several ways to achieve this.

Priority level

One way to suppress notifications is to ask users to set the priority of different checks.

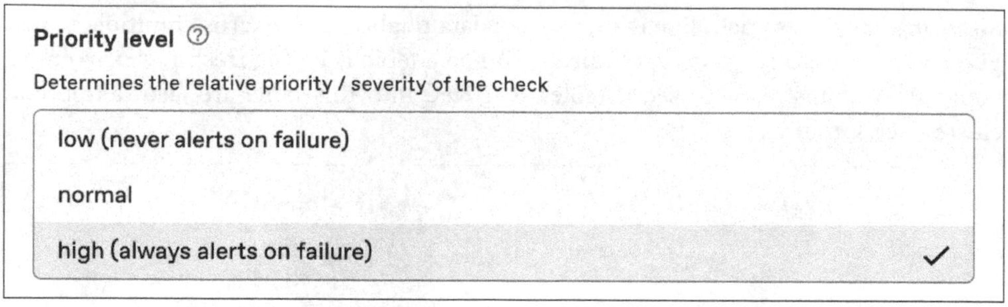

> **Priority level** ⑦
>
> Determines the relative priority / severity of the check
>
> ---
>
> low (never alerts on failure)
>
> normal
>
> high (always alerts on failure)   ✓

Figure 6-7. Priority levels for data quality checks.

As shown in Figure 6-7, we suggest three priority levels: high, normal, and low. The Anomalo platform implements those priorities in the following way, though you may find that you need a different interpretation:

High
> These checks will alert the user every time they fail, as well as the first time they pass following a failure.

Normal
> Normal checks alert the first three times the check fails in a row, suppressing additional repeated alerts. Like high-priority checks, they also alert when they pass again following this failure. Most checks should fall into this priority level, and it's the default for new checks.

Low
> These checks never alert users when they fail. This priority level is useful for debugging data issues or when you want to document a particular type of data quality issue, but you don't want to be notified about it.

Continuous retraining

The ML approach to data quality monitoring that we described in Chapter 4 involves retraining the model every day when new data comes in. This has the advantage of automatically suppressing alerts for "known issues" that might otherwise continue to notify users.

If on day 1 there is a sudden new issue, such as a change in the distribution for a column, the model will alert about it on day 1. But on day 2, we'll retrain the model *using day 1's data*. So, the model essentially recognizes that day 1 represents a "new normal" for this dataset and suppresses alerts for issues that appeared on day 1.

Narrowing the scope of the model

To reduce the number of data quality alerts you receive overall, it can be helpful to narrow the scope of the tables that you monitor with ML to just the ones you really

---

care about. Refer back to Table 3-1 for an example of how ML monitoring is applied to just the important tables in a large data warehouse.

For ML-based approaches that scan the entirety of the table, you can also limit the columns to just those of interest. Data often migrates its schema over time, with new columns added and others deprecated. To avoid causing downstream failures, most systems leave legacy columns in place and always add new columns rather than changing old ones. This can lead to many columns that are deprecated and should be excluded from monitoring, as they may lead to additional notifications that no one needs to care about.

A final very powerful way to narrow the scope of fully automated monitoring is to look at the SQL query logs that are hitting the data warehouse. The SQL queries that are generated by dashboards, machine learning models, or ad hoc analytics queries are all clues as to which data matters the most (we call this *heat* in the data). By parsing those queries and identifying which tables and columns are used the most, automated approaches can be narrowed even further to just the most important data in the organization.

Making the check less sensitive

Finally, it's helpful to give users affordances to manually tune the sensitivity of a given check so that it alerts less frequently. For instance, you can let them widen the range of the acceptable bad values, or they can decide if the monitor should alert only on *new* bad records that appear in a table.

For checks that leverage time series to set ranges dynamically (like the metrics monitoring we discussed in Chapter 2), you can also let users change the confidence interval to make these checks less sensitive, as illustrated in "Metrics Monitoring" on page 29.

Prediction confidence interval ⑦	Prediction alert direction ⑦
The predicted confidence interval width	Alert if a value is above or below the interval
95	both ⌄

Figure 6-8. Confidence interval options for an alert.

The confidence interval can have a large effect on the sensitivity of the notification. Figure 6-9 shows a time series metrics monitoring check with a 95% confidence interval on the left side and an 80% confidence interval on the right side.

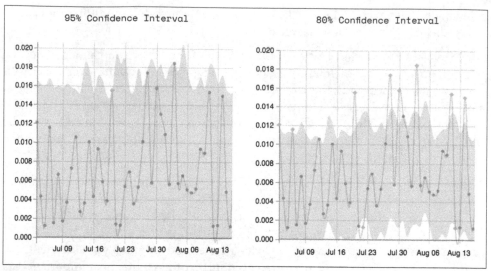

Figure 6-9. Comparing different confidence intervals.

An 80% confidence interval means that, on average, we expect the latest metric value to fall within the confidence interval 80% of the time. That means that it will fall out of the interval 20% of the time. On average, that means you will get an alert every 5 days (1 / .2 = 5).

In contrast, the result will only fall outside of a 99% confidence interval 1% of the time, which means you'd expect an alert every 1 / .01 = 100 days.

Note that in practice, there may be periods of time where alerts happen more frequently, and other long stretches where there are no alerts.

What not to suppress: Expected changes

Sometimes you expect a change in your data. For instance, you might plan to deprecate a column in a certain table, so you expect that all of its values will go to NULL tomorrow. It's natural to think that perhaps you should suppress alerts for these kinds of changes, for example, by supplying a list of expected changes to your monitoring system.

In general, this isn't a good idea. It's quite difficult to maintain a list of expected changes, and it is *very* difficult to map each change to the specific table, column, type of change, and moment when that change will take effect. Without precision in this mapping, you risk either failing to suppress an expected change or suppressing an unexpected change. Both have consequences for trust.

In practice, we've found that it is better to allow expected changes to still trigger data quality checks. The alert will verify that the change did in fact happen and can provide context (root cause analysis, time of day, etc.) that may prove useful. Furthermore, the notification will act as a saved log of the change and its implications, which can be helpful to future analysts, especially if there were any unintended consequences.

Automating the Root Cause Analysis

Usually, before you can resolve a data quality issue, you need to pinpoint the location in the data where the problem is happening. The clock is ticking—as long as the issue remains unresolved, the data scarring will only magnify, costing the business more money and resources as time goes on. But root cause analysis is traditionally very time-consuming, requiring analysts to comb through records and perform custom, complex SQL analyses.

Imagine that you have a data quality check to verify that a certain column is never NULL. Suddenly that check is failing, and you want to figure out where all the NULLs are coming from in a table with millions of records. What if your notifications could be accompanied by an automatic root cause analysis?

One way to achieve this would be to use the unsupervised ML approach described in Chapter 4 to explain the differences between the good and bad rows. In practice, however, users care most about understanding if there is a specific segment in the data that best explains where the bad data is coming from (e.g., a specific geography, type of event, or product line), and they want an explanation that's as clear as possible. We've found that this can be achieved with a much simpler, less computationally intensive approach. Namely, you can sample the data, segment it ("WHERE column = x"), and analyze each data segment independently.

To understand this process, let's start by considering the rectangle in Figure 6-10, which represents all the data. Sections A and B are where the data is passing the check. Sections C and D are where the data is failing the check. The segment of data in question is the B/D area on the right, compared to the rest of the data in the A/C area on the left.

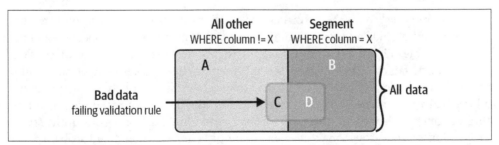

Figure 6-10. How bad data may occur in a table, when looking at a particular segment.

The percentage of bad rows in the segment, compared to bad rows in the total data, is D / (C + D). The percentage of good rows in the segment, compared to good rows in the total data, is B / (A + B). We can then compare these percentages. What we are looking for are samples where the bad rows are highly overrepresented compared to the overall population, and the good rows are highly underrepresented.

To help explain further, Figure 6-11 shows the four categories that a segment could fall into. If a segment contains almost the same proportion of bad data as the entire population (upper left), it's most likely unrelated to the incident. If a segment includes all of the bad data but also a lot of good data (upper right), it may help point us in the right direction, but it's not granular enough to pinpoint the issue. If a segment is mostly bad data but is also missing a lot of the bad data (lower left), it's insufficient to understand the issue. Finally, if a segment contains all of the bad data and hardly anything else (lower right), you've probably found the root cause.

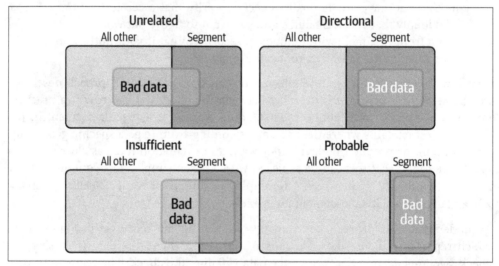

Figure 6-11. Different possible locations for the bad data compared to the segment, and the respective implications.

Since it's pretty fast to do the percentage calculations described earlier, you can automate this and provide a visualization that shows the most likely root cause segments. As an example, Figure 6-12 shows data segments that are likely the root cause of a data check failing (in this case, the table tracks ticket sales, and a concerning number of ticket prices were NULL). The top segment is our likely culprit: it covers all the bad rows and very few of the good rows (the light gray rectangle). The next three segments also cover 100% of the bad rows, but have a significantly higher proportion of good rows, making them more directional rather than probable. The final segment shown, where eventname = "Il Trovatore", is notable because it contains exclusively bad rows. But because it has such a small number of the total bad rows, this segment is insufficient to understand the root cause.

Note that since you're sampling the data anyway and separating it into good and bad rows, you can also make these samples available to explore and/or export for further analysis, as in Figure 6-13.

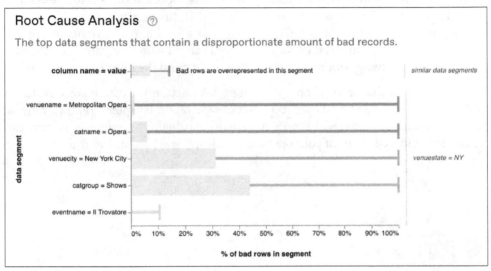

Figure 6-12. Data segments that contain a disproportionate amount of bad records. See a full-sized version of this image at https://oreil.ly/adqm_6_12.

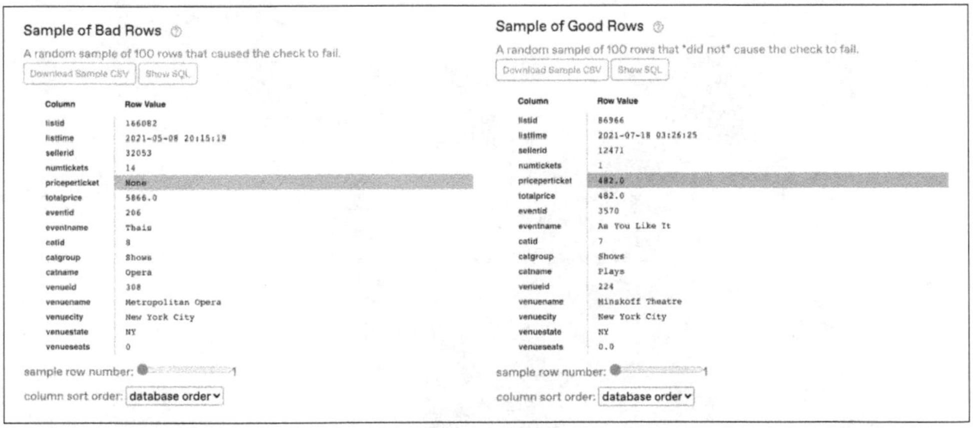

Figure 6-13. Samples of good and bad rows. See a full-sized version of this image at https://oreil.ly/adqm_6_13.

Conclusion

You have many design decisions to make when implementing notifications for an automated data quality monitoring system. It's especially complex when those notifications need to scale across a large data warehouse and multiple teams. We hope this chapter has given you a good starting point for what notifications should contain in order to be actionable, how they can be delivered to the appropriate audience, and where you should think about building in tuning knobs and guardrails to prevent alert fatigue. As you can see, there's a lot that you can do with thoughtful automation, including even helping with root cause analysis right from the notification.

Notifications are the heart of how your users take action on data quality issues to address data shocks and heal data scars. But as we'll see in Chapter 7 on integrations, there are many other ways that an automated data quality monitoring system can extend into different parts of your operations to foster trust around your data.

Integrating Monitoring with Data Tools and Systems

As we discussed in Chapter 1, data quality monitoring doesn't exist in a vacuum—it's a key part of an organization's data stack, which consists of many different systems and components. This means that integrations are an essential part of any data quality monitoring platform. There are two flavors of integrations: table stakes and differentiators. Table stakes integrations with data warehouses/data lakes and ETL tools are necessary for your platform to detect data quality issues for data at rest and data in motion.

Then there are the differentiators: the integrations that aren't necessary to detect data quality problems but add a lot of secondary value. Examples include integrations with data catalogs and analytics or business intelligence (BI) tools. These ensure that when someone is looking at data in a different context, outside of the UX of the data quality fmonitoring platform, they can immediately understand whether that data is high quality.

In this chapter, we'll explore how to integrate with:

- Data warehouses like Snowflake and Databricks
- Data orchestrators like Apache Airflow and dbt
- Data catalogs like Alation and Databricks Unity Catalog
- Data consumers like BI dashboards and machine learning models

We'll explain why you might want to integrate with each category of tool, and we'll walk through the steps needed to integrate successfully. But first, let's take a big-picture look at how data quality monitoring fits into the modern data stack.

Monitoring Your Data Stack

An enterprise's data stack typically consists of the following systems:

- Raw data sources such as events, logs, SaaS apps, and third-party data feeds
- Data storage tools such as cloud data warehouses or data lakes
- Orchestration tools that ETL data from one format into another; for example, to prepare operational data for use in analytics tools
- Data catalogs and governance tools for exploring what data is available, understanding lineage, and auditing changes
- MLOps infrastructure for managing data used specifically for machine learning
- BI and analytics tools for gaining insights from the data

Most businesses want to deploy data quality monitoring not just in one place in their stack, but several. For instance, they may want to have the platform continuously monitor key tables in their data warehouse while also integrating the platform's checks as a task in their orchestration workflow so that a transformation can't be completed if it introduces a data quality issue.

Additionally, there are places in the stack that may benefit from data quality *information*, even if checks aren't actively happening there. For instance, you may want to automatically retrain an ML model if there is a significant shift in data quality. Or you might want BI analysts to be able to see when the data that feeds a dashboard has unresolved quality issues.

While most tools in the data stack expose interfaces for sending and retrieving information, these by and large all look different, and the data itself will be in different formats; there's no standard way of integrating with every data warehouse, for instance. There's been some encouraging movement in the data ecosystem toward standardization for data quality integrations—for example, Alation's Open Data Quality Initiative and dbt's Semantic Layer. That said, integrations still require substantial engineering work and a robust API.

Making matters more difficult, most enterprises haven't settled on a single tool for each part of the data stack. Often, there are independent data teams operating in different business verticals that have evolved to use different sets of tools.

If you're building a data quality monitoring platform in house, you'll want to audit these tools, estimate the amount of time needed to integrate with each, and prioritize your efforts. This might factor into your build versus buy decision (see Chapter 8 for more details). On the other hand, if you are working with a vendor, you will want to ensure they support integrations with the tools you care about, without imposing a large amount of work on your team.

Data Warehouses

Data warehouses (we will use this umbrella term for simplicity; it includes other forms of storage such as data lakes) are a table-stakes integration. It's essential to monitor the data coming into the warehouse, as this is the central source of truth where data is in its intended "at rest" format. Furthermore, the data warehouse feeds downstream data consumers like ML models and analytics dashboards.

Most large enterprises have not standardized around a single data warehouse, and it's usually necessary to support multiple data warehouse integrations. This may include legacy on-premises warehouses (e.g., Teradata) if your business plans to use one indefinitely or is in the process of migrating to the cloud. Many companies will also want to monitor data from their real-time transactional databases (e.g., Postgres, SQL Server, Oracle). Some organizations also choose to use multiple cloud data warehouses (e.g., using both Snowflake and Databricks) to take advantage of their relative strengths.

As we'll discuss in a moment, data quality monitoring with unsupervised ML is especially useful when an organization has multiple data warehouses, because it can check that data is accurately replicated across those warehouses.

Integrating with Data Warehouses

The details of the backend integration will vary depending on the data warehouse. Most data sources support SQL-based querying, which is often the API through which the data is tested, statistics are computed, or samples are extracted from the underlying data. However, the SQL dialects can vary dramatically, and the SQL required for the rules, statistics, or samples will also need to vary and be tested on each supported platform.

In addition, different platforms have different scalability requirements—for example, in Presto, it is critically important to include a time-based WHERE SQL filter in every query. In BigQuery, there is not an unbiased way to sample data at random without scanning a large number of rows. Legacy or transactional data stores may not respond well to the query load from automated monitoring, and the monitoring system may need to be robust to short query time-outs or long query queues; in this case, optimization of the SQL queries becomes paramount.

In general, users will need the following to enable monitoring:

Network connectivity
> You may need to add the IPs for your monitoring application to the allowlist for your data warehouse.

Read-access credentials on the database

We recommend creating a dedicated service account for monitoring with read-only access to the tables you want to monitor.

Beyond this, for many traditional warehouses, users should only need to provide the host, port, database name, user ID, and password. Snowflake just requires an account ID and database name, as shown in Figure 7-1. To connect to Databricks, users will need to generate a personal access token (*https://oreil.ly/C8UZR*).

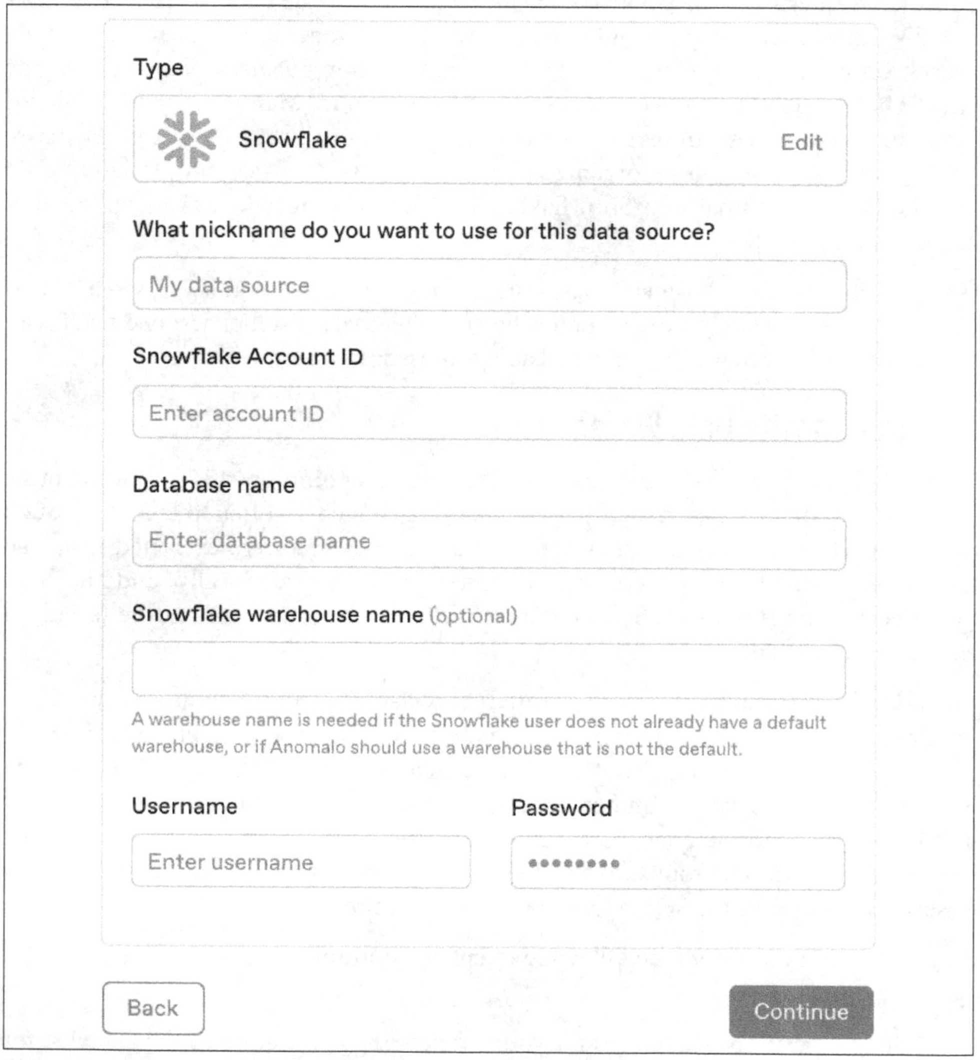

Figure 7-1. Setting up a Snowflake integration.

With the appropriate access, on the backend, you'll need to set up processes that scan the data warehouse for every queryable object that the credentials have access to, including tables, views, and materialized views. These objects should be organized and presented to users so that they can configure tables for monitoring. See Figure 7-2.

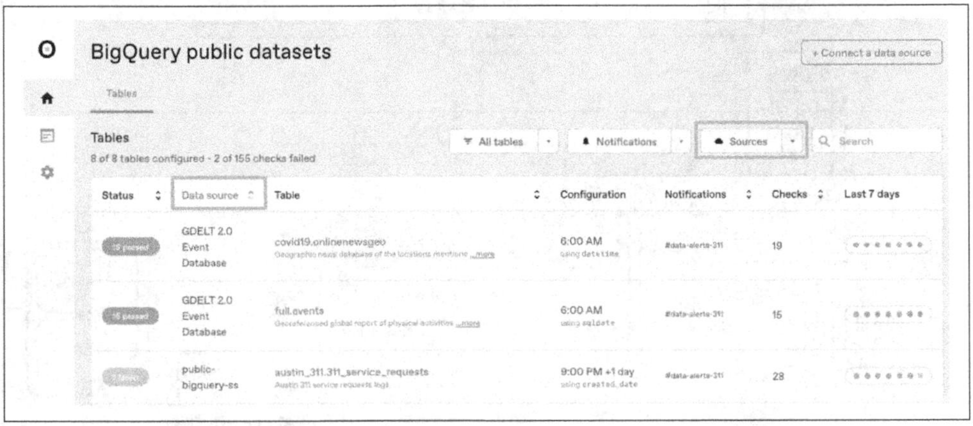

Figure 7-2. Filtering by data source. See a full-sized version of this image at https://oreil.ly/adqm_7_2.

As described in Chapter 2, it's also important to extract metadata from the data warehouse, such as when a table was last updated and what the volume of the last update was, which is useful for observability. The metadata is also used for lineage, which is useful for root cause analysis. Modern cloud data warehouses will expose much of this information via API, such as the Databricks data lineage API (*https://oreil.ly/zTimS*). It's much more cost-effective to extract and track metadata than it is to run unsupervised ML on the entire data warehouse, so, as we've touched on elsewhere in the book, most organizations will monitor the majority of tables using metadata-based observability, saving deep data quality monitoring for their most important tables.

How often should you scan for new objects and metadata in the data warehouse? We recommend running this process daily to detect new tables and changes to table schema, as this mirrors the frequency at which most data quality checks will occur. If you anticipate scenarios where you will want to make updates and see those reflected in the tool in real time, it may be useful to provide a way for users to manually trigger a data warehouse refresh (e.g., via a REST endpoint).

To illustrate further, Figure 7-3 shows a simplified example of how the Anomalo architecture integrates with all the other systems in a typical deployment and clearly delineates what runs inside of the data quality monitoring platform (the dashed box). The platform itself can run on a single virtual machine using Open Container

Initiative (OCI) containers (e.g., via Docker) or, to facilitate horizontal scaling, can be deployed on a Kubernetes cluster using a Helm chart.

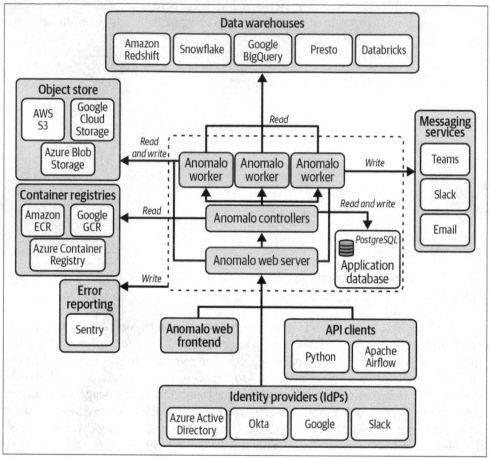

Figure 7-3. A simplified example of how the Anomalo architecture integrates with all the other systems in a typical deployment.

Starting from the bottom, users interact with the platform via a web frontend or API clients, secured via single sign-on (SSO) integrations with enterprise identity providers (IdPs) and API keys. The web frontend provides rich graphical user interfaces for interacting with the platform from the browser and communicates with the web server via HTTPS.

The web server responds to all the external requests from SSO, APIs, or browser sessions via HTTPS. Backend controllers then create jobs that are queued and scheduled for execution. There is a dynamic pool of workers that can pick up those jobs and process them (these could be metadata retrieval tasks, SQL queries, check logic, or ML jobs).

All of these internal systems maintain a shared state in an internal database (we use Postgres). This database can itself be hosted inside of the environment (in Docker or Kubernetes) or can be a managed Postgres service like AWS RDS.

The bulk of the action takes place in the workers that are performing the checks. Those workers will send notifications to external channels (e.g., Slack, Microsoft Teams, PagerDuty) and read from the data warehouses, data lakes, or databases that are being monitored (e.g., Snowflake, Databricks, BigQuery, Amazon Redshift).

They will also write large objects they process, such as samples of record-level data or visualizations they produce, into a cloud object store such as AWS S3. In a typical deployment, this is a file storage bucket that the customer controls.

When runtime errors are encountered by any of the workers, they write information about the exception to an external platform like Sentry, which is used to debug the exception (without including any of the customer data).

Finally, the entire platform can be upgraded automatically. A controller monitors the Anomalo container registry for a new deployment tagged to a specific customer or environment and then automatically upgrades all of the internal components in a safe and reliable way.

Security

Perhaps it goes without saying, but we'll say it anyway: when you integrate with a business data source, you take on a significant responsibility to protect that data, which could contain personally identifiable information (PII) and other sensitive information. Depending on your use case, you may need to conform to certain compliance and legal requirements around data processing (see an example of our data processing agreement (*https://oreil.ly/vCTzJ*)).

When developing a solution for third-party customers, there are milestones you should aim for with respect to data security. SOC 2 certification is the industry standard for service providers storing customer data in the cloud. Developed by the AICPA (*https://oreil.ly/dEz8X*), SOC 2 is an extensive auditing procedure that ensures that a company is handling customer data securely and in a manner that protects the organization as well as the privacy of its customers.

Reconciling Data Across Multiple Warehouses

When your organization leverages multiple data storage solutions, you often have duplicate data represented in more than one place and want to ensure that the data is the same in both tables. One example is ensuring that data is the same before and after a migration.

Monitoring to ensure that data is the same usually takes two forms: either rule-based testing or unsupervised machine learning.

Comparing datasets with rule-based testing

If two tables are identical across two data warehouses, there are three conditions that must be true:

- The schemas are the same. The tables must have the same columns, with the same types, in the same order.
- The set of primary keys are the same. The tables' rows must join one-to-one on the primary keys.
- Each row has the same values. When joined on the primary keys, the values in both tables' rows must be the same.

If all three of these are true, then the two tables must have entirely identical rows. Between the two, there's no data that has been added, duplicated, lost, or modified.

However, the rule-based testing approach requires the data to be in the same data warehouse, such that joins between the tables can be evaluated at scale. This is impractical for very large datasets and introduces a risk of false positives caused by issues in the ETL process to move the data into the same data warehouse platform.

Comparing datasets with unsupervised machine learning

In Chapter 4, we discussed how the unsupervised ML approach for data quality monitoring can also be used to compare two datasets on demand. In this case, you would sample data from tables in the respective data warehouses, then train a model to predict whether data came from warehouse A or warehouse B. By explaining the model's predictions using SHAP values, you can pinpoint and root-cause the differences in the sample data.

While this approach may not catch *every* row-level issue like a rule will, it scales to massive datasets and allows you to compare data from different source data warehouses without any ETL process.

Comparing summary statistics

The final approach for comparing two tables is to compute some summary statistics about each table and then compare those statistics to ensure that they are identical. For example, you might compute the number of rows and average price grouped by product category to compare that product price listing data was consistently replicated from one environment to another. This has the advantage of being very scalable and allowing you to ensure that the data is identical in some small ways. But it cannot compare all the records in the table if the table is large.

In practice, we've found a combination of the latter two approaches—ensuring the row counts and some key statistics are identical when aggregated, and ensuring there are no significant distribution differences using ML when drawing samples—is the most scalable and reliable way to reconcile datasets across platforms.

Data Orchestrators

Different business users will want to see or perform data quality checks in different places. In some cases, they'll want to do data quality checks while the data is in flight—in other words, undergoing ingestion and transformation—before it gets to the "at rest" state in your data warehouse. Sometimes, they'll want to perform data quality checks even before the data enters the data warehouse at all.

This is where orchestrators and ETL tools like Apache Airflow, dbt, Fivetran, Databricks Workflows, or Prefect come in.

Integrating with Orchestrators

The standard pattern for integrating with an orchestration or workflow tool is to create jobs that allow your monitoring solution to slot into the data orchestration DAG. Put simply, the DAG is a series of tasks that complete in a particular order, with upstream and downstream dependencies.

A common DAG is to first extract data from the appropriate sources, for example, from user logs and a staging environment. These could be the independent tasks that kick off the DAG, as seen in Figure 7-4. After completing both tasks, data can be merged and transformed into the desired format before finally being loaded into the desired place for storage. Orchestration tools automate and schedule this process, giving visibility into when a given task completes or fails.

By integrating your monitoring platform with an orchestration tool, you can run checks at essentially any point in the DAG. For instance, you might want to run checks after the transformation stage, or after the data extraction stage (or both).

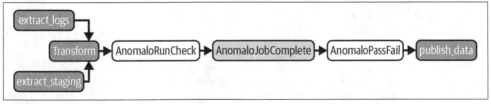

Figure 7-4. An example data orchestration DAG that includes data quality checks before publishing data.

We recommend that you support three types of functions at a minimum:

Run checks

Connect to your monitoring solution and run the checks that have been configured for the table. In Figure 7-4, this is `AnomaloRunCheck`.

Job sensor

You will need some way to determine when your monitoring system has finished running checks. We do this via a polling method. In Figure 7-4, this is `Anomalo JobComplete`.

Validate checks

This allows the user to decide whether they care about all of the checks passing or only some of them. Once we get the output of the checks, we can ensure that if we have failed any "must-pass" checks, we raise an exception that stops the workflow from completing and triggers a notification to the user. In Figure 7-4, this step is `AnomaloPassFail`.

Often, it's useful to package this functionality into a library for users of the ETL tool. The code behind these functions is not particularly complex. Here is an example of an Airflow operator for running checks:

```
# Importing BaseOperator for creating custom operators in Airflow.
from airflow.operators import BaseOperator

# Importing AnomaloHook to interact with Anomalo API.
from anomalo import AnomaloHook


class AnomaloRunCheckOperator(BaseOperator):
    def __init__(self,
                 table_name,
                 anomalo_conn_id="anomalo_default",
                 *args,
                 **kwargs):
        super().__init__(*args, **kwargs)
        self.anomalo_conn_id = anomalo_conn_id
        self.table_name = table_name

    def execute(self, context):
        # Creating an API client.
        api_client = AnomaloHook(
            anomalo_conn_id=self.anomalo_conn_id
            ).get_client()
        # Fetching the table_id corresponding to the table name.
        table_id = api_client.get_table_information(
            table_name=self.table_name
            )["id"]
        # Triggering the run checks operation in Anomalo and getting job ID.
        run = api_client.run_checks(table_id=table_id)
```

```
        # Logging the information about the triggered checks.
        self.log.info(f"Triggered Anomalo checks for {self.table_name}")
        # Returning the job ID for the triggered run.
        return run["run_checks_job_id"]
```

AnomaloRunCheckOperator triggers a job that runs all of the checks on a given table. table_name is the full name of the table in Anomalo, and anomalo_conn_id is the connection ID to connect to the platform.

The next file we'll walk through sets up an example Airflow DAG that ingests data and then runs checks on it using AnomaloRunCheckOperator.

We start by importing the Airflow modules and classes required to define a DAG, as well as custom Anomalo operators and sensors:

```
from airflow.models import DAG
from airflow.operators.empty import EmptyOperator
from airflow.utils.dates import days_ago

from airflow.providers.anomalo.operators.anomalo import (
    AnomaloPassFailOperator,
    AnomaloRunCheckOperator,
)
from airflow.providers.anomalo.sensors.anomalo import AnomaloJobCompleteSensor
```

Next, we define default arguments for DAG tasks and we set up basic parameters for the DAG:

```
# Default arguments for DAG tasks.
args = {
    "owner": "AL",
    "start_date": days_ago(1),
}

# Define the DAG using context manager.
with DAG(
    dag_id="AnomaloDAG",  # Unique identifier for the DAG.
    default_args=args,  # Default task arguments.
    description="Simple Anomalo Airflow operator example",  # DAG description.
    schedule_interval="@daily",  # Frequency of DAG execution.
) as dag:
```

The DAG consists of several tasks. There is ingest_transform_data, the initial task to bring in the data and do some operations on it. Once we do that, we'll want to have a task that can run checks on a table using AnomaloRunCheckOperator. Note that the following steps are all indented, as they are happening inside of the Airflow DAG context manager:

```
        # Initial task to ingest and transform data.
        ingest_transform_data = EmptyOperator(task_id="ingest_transform_data")

        # Task to run checks on a specific table using AnomaloRunCheckOperator.
```

```
anomalo_run = AnomaloRunCheckOperator(
    task_id="AnomaloRunCheck",
    table_name="public-bq.crypto_bitcoin.outputs",
)
```

As discussed previously, we want to poll until the Anomalo job is complete, and we do this with the `anomalo_sensor` task:

```
anomalo_sensor = AnomaloJobCompleteSensor(
    task_id="AnomaloJobCompleteSensor",
    # Reference to the previous task's job ID.
    xcom_job_id_task=anomalo_run.task_id,
    poke_interval=60,
    timeout=900,  # 15 minutes
    mode="poke",
)
```

When the job is complete, we will run a task to validate various data quality checks and finally publish the data:

```
anomalo_validate = AnomaloPassFailOperator(
    task_id="AnomaloPassFail",
    table_name="public-bq.crypto_bitcoin.outputs",
    must_pass=[
        "data_freshness",
        "data_volume",
        "metric",
        "rule",
        "missing_data",
        "anomaly",
    ],
)
```

```
publish_data = EmptyOperator(task_id="publish_data")
```

With these tasks defined, it's just a matter of setting up task dependencies to form the DAG:

```
(
    ingest_transform_data
    >> anomalo_run
    >> anomalo_sensor
    >> anomalo_validate
    >> publish_data
)
```

Data Catalogs

Since many enterprises today are working with vast volumes of diverse datasets, data catalogs are becoming an increasingly essential part of a data practitioner's toolkit. A data catalog provides a centralized view of data assets, metadata, and relationships, making it easier to discover, understand, and use data across an organization. Examples include Alation, Databricks Unity Catalog, DataHub, and Atlan.

Integrations between data catalogs and data quality tools are a natural evolution—a result of enterprises realizing that understanding their data and ensuring that their data is high quality are interrelated goals. Both of these steps can be seen as part of data governance, which is a framework that defines the policies, processes, and standards for managing data assets across an organization. It ensures data is properly accessible, protected, and trusted to meet the needs of the organization and its stakeholders.

 As an example of the continuing push for more connections between data quality tools and data catalogs, in 2022, Alation launched the Open Data Quality Initiative (*https://oreil.ly/ RSXVI*), which "offers an open DQ API, developer documentation, onboarding, integration best practices, and comarketing support." They added a Data Quality tab to the catalog (see Figure 7-5), where data quality systems can push information via API.

Overview	Columns 17	Samples...	Filters 10	Joins 7	Lineage	Queries 9	Health ⚠ 2

Data Health

Data Quality 2   ⚠ **Data Quality**

	Object Name	Status ↓	Value ↓↑	Description ↓↑
Comparing queries 'Low score last 7 day...' ⊡	⊞ cstmr_dems	⚠	rule	There are severe differences in the data wh...
timestamp is never NULL ⊡	⊞ cstmr_dems	⚠	rule	timestamp has 26,818 (0.1%) NULL values, ...
is fresh ⊡	⊞ cstmr_dems	⊘	data_freshness	has 2,890 rows on 2022-05-09

Tooltip: Comparing queries 'Low score last 7 days' and 'High score last 7 days' using machine learning

Figure 7-5. As part of their Open Data Quality Initiative, Alation added hooks for showing data quality checks. See a full-sized version of this image at https://oreil.ly/ adqm_7_5.

Integrations between catalogs and data quality monitoring can be bidirectional. Inside the catalog, it's very helpful to be able to see information about data quality right next to information about the table, without having to switch contexts. Alternatively, from within the monitoring platform, it can also be useful to have deep links into the catalog to explore table usage and metadata.

Showing detailed data quality information inside the catalog (see Figure 7-6) is powerful for several reasons. A data catalog is often a business's go-to tool for exploring datasets that might be helpful for a particular use case, such as developing a new analytics dashboard. At this stage, an analyst might be choosing from hundreds of tables that they don't know anything about. It's essential to understand if the data in a given table is any good: Is it valid and approved, or has it never been tested? Having data quality details right at an analyst's fingertips can ensure that the business makes decisions backed by trustworthy information.

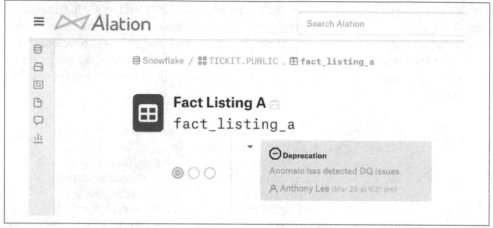

Figure 7-6. Data quality checks appear in the catalog's overview for a table, and any issues are flagged in the UI.

Additionally, one of the jobs of a data catalog is to not only collate assets but to tell the business which ones are the most popular and commonly used. By integrating data quality information into the catalog, it's possible to quickly see which of the popular tables are actually validated. If a manager is running an initiative to improve data quality, this can be very helpful for prioritizing where to invest resources. Overall, it serves as a gauge of whether the business is operating on trustworthy data.

Integrating with Catalogs

A baseline integration with a data catalog involves tagging whether tables have checks or monitoring set up at all, showing the results of data quality checks in the catalog, and deep linking to the monitoring platform for more information.

However, more advanced integrations are becoming possible as catalogs add increased support for data quality tools to plug in. For instance, if your monitoring tool provides additional visualizations (e.g., root cause analysis), you might consider bringing those into the catalog as well.

Generally, integrating with data catalogs follows a publishing model where the data quality monitor will aggregate its results and publish them to a designated location that is owned by the catalog. The integration is primarily API based, so it's important to have a secure and enterprise-ready API.

For instance, you can provide a REST API that returns monitoring results as JSON. Endpoints might include:

`GET /get_checks_for_table`
> Return a list of all currently configured checks/validations for a given table ID.

`POST /run_checks`
> Manually run all or a subset of checks on a given table.

`GET /get_run_results`
> Obtain the results of executed checks from a single run.

For a `GET /get_run_results` call, check metadata you might want to provide includes:

- Check ID: identifier for a specific data check
- Check run ID: identifier for an instance of a check run
- Completion time: when the check run was completed
- Creation metadata: information about who created the check and when
- Last edited metadata: information about the last edit, including time and editor
- Error status: whether the check encountered an error
- Evaluation message: text detailing the check evaluation
- Exception details: messages and traceback for any exceptions
- Historical context: summary of the check's performance over time
- Sample data: SQL queries and URLs for good and bad data samples
- Result statistics: quantitative metrics and their names, related to the check
- Success flag: Boolean indicating the check's success or failure
- Check configuration: including type, description, and priority level
- Triage status: current status in the triage workflow

The trickiest part of the integration, in our experience, is matching table IDs correctly, as table names aren't always a perfect identifier (they may be represented slightly differently for different data catalogs) and every enterprise's environment will be slightly different.

You'll also need to think about scheduling: How often do you want to push results to the catalog and/or pull updates from the catalog? As a first step, you can run updates using a script and eventually build a scheduler into your platform to automate the process daily or on some other cadence.

Data Consumers

Though still nascent, another area where data quality integrations are powerful—and likely to become more popular—is applications that consume data, such as BI and analytics tools and MLOps platforms.

Analytics and BI Tools

An analytics tool like Tableau, because it serves as the destination where data is used, would be a good candidate for showing data quality monitoring information, such as whether the dataset that powers a dashboard has been validated as high quality. In fact, Tableau has several data quality APIs, such as an API to add a data quality warning (*https://oreil.ly/2zMbN*). If you use BI dashboards to track KPIs, consider syncing this metric monitoring with your data quality tool so that you can easily root cause any drift in the underlying data.

Data-driven organizations often run into the problem of inconsistent definitions for their business metrics. For instance, one part of the business might define `view_count` as excluding very short views, say those less than 10 milliseconds in duration, while another group might include all views, leading to what appears to be a data quality issue—but it's really just a lack of consistency.

We've been interested in how dbt is tackling this problem with the launch of dbt metrics and the dbt Semantic Layer. This allows organizations to centrally define key business metrics like revenue, customer count, and churn rate in dbt. It's possible for data quality monitoring tools to be dbt "Metrics Ready integrations" and use dbt metrics definitions. For instance, if your tool monitors KPIs, you can automatically ingest the metrics that have been defined in dbt.

MLOps

If your company is using an MLOps platform like Amazon SageMaker, most likely you already have some level of model monitoring built in. However, most platforms monitor metrics like model performance, latency, and uptime rather than the harder-to-detect issues of incorrect data flowing into models and resulting in suboptimal predictions. By integrating data quality monitoring with MLOps tools, you could build a system that warns data scientists when models need to be retrained because the underlying data has drifted, or when there are errors like NULLs in the data that could cause a model to behave erratically.

Figure 7-7 is an example MLOps architecture diagram adapted from the Google Cloud Architecture Center.

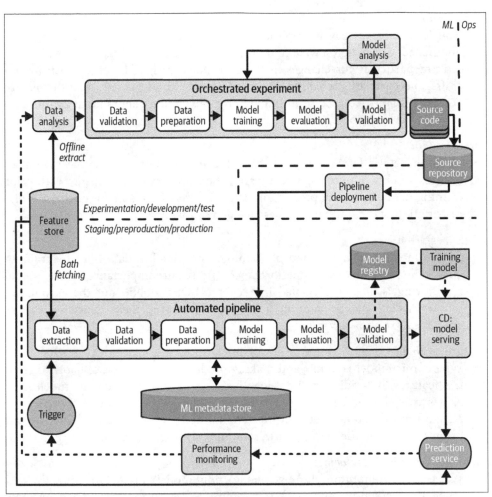

Figure 7-7. Example MLOps architecture diagram (adapted from "MLOps: Continuous Delivery and Automation Pipelines in Machine Learning," Cloud Architecture Center, https://oreil.ly/rfAmt).

This complex flow is designed to automate the continuous integration, delivery, and training of ML systems. Here are the points where you might want to introduce data quality monitoring:

Source data

Source data, typically from a cloud data warehouse or data lake, is transformed into signals for the model that are then stored in the feature store. It's essential to monitor this data as it's the entry point for training ML models.

Feature store

The feature store may be replicated in your data warehouse, and this is yet another set of tables you want to monitor. As discussed in Chapter 3, you should look in particular for changes in the percentage of NULL values, distribution shifts, and correlation changes. Any of these could indicate risks that the feature computation is incorrect, or the model might experience shocks that could cause unexpected behavior.

Training data

Training data is fetched in batch from the feature store. It may be helpful to use data quality monitoring to compare the current training snapshot with prior training datasets or with production data. You may have some model risk if the distribution of the training data has changed suddenly.

Model performance

In the model evaluation step of training, you can log data like the training and inference times, test set performance, and feature importance scores. Model monitoring is ideally integrated into your MLOps toolkit, but there's nothing to stop a data quality platform from also monitoring these metrics if they're available in your data warehouse.

Feature serving

When your model is online and making predictions, it can be valuable to fetch the features at prediction time, log them, and compare them to the feature values used for the latest training run. This can tell you if you're experiencing a significant difference between the training and real-world data, which would mean that your model may perform suboptimally in production.

Predictions and business logic

While you can monitor your machine learning model's predictions directly, we'd argue it's even more important to monitor the *business logic driven by those predictions*. For instance, are you suddenly marking a large percentage of transactions as fraudulent? This may indicate that there is a real trend in the external data, but it might also mean that your model is performing erratically due to a data quality issue.

Conclusion

When you automate data quality monitoring at scale, you create ways to validate whether that data is high quality (or not). Notifications are the main way to resolve data quality issues, but to really get users across your organization engaging with your system—and with data quality as a whole at your company—you have to go beyond notifications and integrate information and signals from your monitoring into your entire data workflow. In this chapter, we've given you the tools to do so.

## CHAPTER 8

Operating Your Solution at Scale

In this final chapter, we'll discuss the challenges you'll likely face as you put an automated data quality monitoring solution into operation and maintain it for the long term. We'll focus on clearly defining the problems, allowing your use case and needs to point you toward the approach that's right for your team.

Operating a technology solution like automated data quality monitoring follows a general pattern. First, there's the process of acquiring the platform, either by building it yourself or purchasing it from a third party. Then, there's the initial configuration and enablement so that your team can use all the features of the platform successfully. Once everything is up and running, the "final" stage is the ongoing use of the platform to facilitate your organization's goals—in this case, improving and maintaining data quality in the long term. We've structured this chapter to follow these phases in order. Now, let's dive in and see how you can reach a steady state of data quality excellence.

Build Versus Buy

Once an organization comprehensively understands a problem they are having and has researched the options in the solution space, they have a decision to make: build or buy?

Building doesn't have to mean building from scratch, and rarely does. A common strategy that small teams may take is to build their own platform around open source packages for rule-based data quality evaluation, such as Great Expectations or Deequ. There are advantages to having complete control over the road map of the data quality initiative:

- You'll be able to fine-tune your ML model for the metrics you care most about.

- You can design notifications and visualizations from the UX point of view of your company.

- If you've built other internal systems for managing data, like a bespoke data catalog, it may be easier to make your DIY data quality monitoring platform compatible with these systems than to integrate with a vendor.

- You'll be in full control of optimizing the costs, runtime, and other performance characteristics of your platform.

- You can build exactly the features you need, including custom functionality that vendors may not offer.

- You won't pay for anything you don't need.

On the other hand, the downsides of the DIY approach often dissuade businesses from going this route, even when they have large teams of engineers:

- You'll need to devote time away from your business's core competency to focus on building a complex platform driven by a sophisticated ML model. This often includes hiring talented engineers and data scientists who may be interested in building the shiny new thing, but not as keen on sticking around to maintain it.

- Different teams at a large enterprise may all build their own bespoke solutions using different technologies. It will be hard to integrate these and have the same transparency into data quality in different parts of the organization.

- Your team will be responsible for 24/7 support and maintenance of the platform, in addition to training and onboarding new users.

- The data landscape is constantly changing. To keep up, you'll need to continue to innovate on your platform over time, adding new features and iterating on your model.

- Vendors specialize in optimizing performance and costs for a data quality monitoring platform—it's core to their business. Unless your engineers are highly experienced and motivated, you may end up with suboptimal metrics.

- Often, homegrown systems will just generate emails that won't be acted upon. In addition to just detecting data quality issues, you'll need to design a sophisticated UX with visualizations to make notifications actionable and help with root cause analysis. This is often the point where the business realizes that the project is too complex to tackle internally.

As the vendor ecosystem for data quality monitoring has grown, the buy option is becoming more and more attractive for enterprises that don't already specialize in building data platforms. The total cost to operate is often less than if the business were responsible for all development and maintenance. With a vendor, businesses can get started right away on advancing the quality of their data rather than waiting for an internal platform to be built out, which typically takes a year or more.

 Cloud data warehouses are increasingly adding data quality monitoring features for enterprises. This makes sense, and you should evaluate what they offer against your top vendor choices. Keep in mind that data warehouses and data lakes, by definition, don't specialize in data quality monitoring and so may not be incentivized to innovate on the problem, provide the best user experience, or address edge case requirements.

An additional concern that many teams have here is lock-in. They may be using several data warehouses/data lakes and don't want to have to consult multiple places for data quality. Or if there's a chance they want to migrate their data later on, they're concerned about the switching cost of reproducing all their rules, checks, notifications, and processes in a new platform.

Vendor Deployment Models

One of the main concerns that businesses have with external vendors is security and data privacy. That's why it's essential to pay attention to a vendor's deployment model, as this greatly affects how much your data is protected. There are three options in general (some vendors might offer only one, or several), and they vary greatly in terms of the security and control you'll have over the platform.

SaaS

The simplest approach to data quality monitoring with a vendor is to use a SaaS deployment. This can be as straightforward as signing up on the company's website, adding a credit card for payment, and entering in credentials that you would like to use for accessing your cloud data warehouse.

However, a SaaS deployment model introduces serious security and privacy risks. The SaaS platform will need to have unfettered read access to the data you wish to monitor. Even if the solution is only using summary statistics to detect data quality issues, samples of data will be needed to help root cause the issue. What's more, many organizations are concerned about sharing metadata from their warehouse, as tables and column names may provide strategic or competitive intelligence that is not public. For large organizations, this kind of exposure is usually a nonstarter.

Fully in-VPC or on-prem

On the other end of the spectrum from SaaS, a fully inside virtual private cloud (in-VPC) or on-premises (on-prem) deployment of a monitoring solution means that the entire monitoring application runs inside a secure cloud or on-prem environment controlled by the customer.

New technologies like Docker and Kubernetes make managing and scaling these in-VPC deployments much easier than they have been in the past. Upgrades can still happen automatically, without the customer having to be involved. For example, new releases can be published to a Docker registry with tags indicating which customer they are appropriate for. Then an automated service that runs inside the application will look for new tags for the deployment and autoupgrade the deployment. Refer back to Figure 7-3 for more details.

Fully in-VPC or on-prem environments can be configured for a range of security postures:

Remote access allowed versus disallowed
It's usually beneficial for the customer to allow the vendor to remotely access the deployment, to help provide a higher quality level of support and to assist in any configuration or issue resolution. However, that may not be possible (or may require contractor relationships) if particularly sensitive data is being stored in the warehouse.

No egress of any information
The most sensitive customers may want to block all data from leaving the deployment. This means everything; for example, the vendor will not get exception reporting or any telemetry from the system. This can significantly increase the monitoring and maintenance burden on the customer and the fees required for deployment or support from the vendor.

Most enterprises and security and privacy-conscious customers opt for fully in-VPC deployments. It's worth noting that in-VPC is a more complicated option from an administrative perspective—if your organization isn't used to managing such deployments, you may be in for a learning curve at the start. But for many companies, the investment of time and resources is worth it to have complete control over where your data and metadata is stored and processed. Full in-VPC is the only way to guarantee that control.

Hybrid

Between the extremes of SaaS and in-VPC, there's a third path. Hybrid solutions try to combine the best of SaaS and in-VPC by having the query and data analysis layer sit inside of the customer's environment (in-VPC), while the presentation and user interaction layers remain in the vendor's cloud (SaaS).

However, given the nature of data quality monitoring, this isn't all that different from SaaS. The customer's data will still frequently leave their environment. Summary statistics and samples of data will need to be presented to users for the tool to provide important transparency and context around data quality issues. And metadata, too, will need to be exposed, even if just to describe the tables and columns that users are examining in the interface.

In practice, we've found that hybrid solutions have to compromise in one of two ways: either they have to hamstring the user experience or they risk exposing sensitive data outside the customer's environment.

Table 8-1 shows these deployment models.

Table 8-1. Vendor deployment models

Deployment model	Query and data analysis layer	Presentation and user interaction layer	Deployment complexity	Can your data be exposed to the vendor?
SaaS	In their environment	In their environment	Least complex	Yes
Hybrid	In your environment	In their environment	Some complexity	Yes
Fully in-VPC	In your environment	In your environment	Most complex	No

Configuration

As with any complex technical solution, the data quality monitoring platform that you build or buy will likely have a range of options that need to be specified at initialization. If you work with large volumes of data, configuration decisions like what tables you monitor and what data you check within those tables are especially important. Your decisions here can protect you from skyrocketing data warehouse costs or vendor fees and ensure that your solution continues to perform well even for tables with billions of records.

With these concerns in mind, we'll walk through the questions most enterprises have when setting up their solution:

- How to determine which tables are most important
- How to decide what specific data in a table to monitor
- How to avoid having to manually configure everything

Determining Which Tables Are Most Important

While it's possible to implement broad observability across your entire warehouse using table metadata alone, automated checks that query the actual *values* of the data are more computationally intensive to run. Therefore, it's usually best to identify which tables matter most and configure only those tables for "deep" data quality monitoring. (See Table 3-1 for an example of how this breaks down at many companies.) Starting with the most important data will also help you onboard team members more quickly and build trust in the tool before expanding its usage.

How do you identify these essential tables? For smaller organizations, it may be obvious to the data team which tables matter the most. For large organizations, that knowledge may be distributed throughout the organization and more difficult to collect and maintain over time. Often, the people who care the most about the quality of the data in a table are the consumers of that data. A tool that makes it easy for the people with the deepest subject matter expertise in a table to set up monitoring enhances an organization's ability to be agile in deciding which tables to monitor.

You might also want to look at SQL query logs from your data warehouse. You can thus determine which tables (and columns and segments) are queried most frequently by automated systems, ad hoc analyst queries, or BI reporting platforms. This "heat" is a great proxy for the most important data.

Deciding What Data in a Table to Monitor

For large tables (especially billions of rows), it can be very expensive to monitor the entirety of the table on a frequent basis. To keep the solution cost-effective, your platform should monitor only the most recent data. If you always query for just the most recent period of time (the data from the previous day is usually sufficient, though sometimes a higher frequency is required), your monitoring will place far less load on the underlying data warehouse, saving money and runtime.

In most cases, you'll still be covered if you monitor recent data only, because the majority of causes of data quality issues happen only to the newest data arriving into a table. There are of course exceptions, such as when historical data is updated in place, and different monitoring strategies are needed for these tables, as discussed in "Updated-in-Place Tables" on page 94.

To monitor the freshest data, you need to partition the data by time. While this might sound straightforward, it can be quite complex, in some cases due to data warehouse requirements, or as a by-product of the data's origin. For a taste of the many different time partitioning schemes we've encountered, see Figure 4-3.

An extra wrinkle: Some tables may not have a time column that can be used to identify the "most recent" records. In this case, there's no real option other than having the automated monitoring system check the entirety of the table each time it is updated and build up snapshots of data to compare changes in the table over time.

Configuration at Scale

If you have 10,000 tables, it doesn't make sense to have someone go through the UI and configure each one by hand. In addition, you may have hundreds or thousands of existing custom data quality rules and checks (in dbt, for example) that you may want to migrate to your new automated platform.

This is another reason, alongside those mentioned in Chapter 6, that your data quality solution should include a robust API with hooks to configure tables for monitoring and add, delete, or update custom checks programmatically. A CLI can be particularly helpful here, as well as the ability to specify configurations via YAML files.

When configurations are specified programmatically, they can be maintained in a version control system like Git. For critical data, this may be helpful for auditing purposes or for ensuring checks are reviewed and approved through a code-review process before being applied to production.

That said, you can't expect to lock down and control all configurations programmatically. You'll need to also allow users to make adjustments and add checks to tables as needed, including business users who may not be comfortable with writing code. So, we suggest that you provide two options: configuration by code as well as self-service configuration via a UI.

Enablement

Both during and after your initial configuration, you'll be introducing your monitoring platform to many different types of stakeholders and, most likely, multiple teams as well. The more people who use the tool, the more people will be invested in improving data quality at your organization. This is a great thing, but it comes with the challenges of managing a large, diverse user base. In this section, we'll describe best practices you can implement for a successful enablement.

User Roles and Permissions

Different systems will have different roles and permissions for their software. For example, a vendor solution might have admins who can fully configure tables, down to viewers who can only look at the results of data quality checks.

It's best to define these roles and permissions very early on. Who will be given the admin roles, and will there be a backup if they go on leave? Will each team have its own admin, or will one person be responsible for all of the configuration? What role will new users get by default when they join a team? If someone has a problem with access, how do they escalate this?

Additionally, you may want to think about whether different teams or divisions within an organization should be siloed in terms of what tables they can access in your tool. It's safest to give access only to what a user needs. For example, not all users will need access to sensitive tables containing HR information.

Onboarding, Training, and Support

Rolling out your data quality monitoring platform to your organization requires careful forethought and planning, and there are many different paths you might take. For example, you could make data quality a top-down initiative that's scaled across dozens of teams right away. On the other hand, you could start small, focus on making one or two teams successful, and push for a viral adoption across your organization driven by early successes. We've seen both approaches work—the right choice depends on your culture, the urgency of your need, how many resources you have, and how closely connected the teams are.

Regardless of the details, we have seen the following general strategies help businesses onboard new groups of employees, train them to be successful, and ensure users are supported in the long term:

Initial kickoff and requirements gathering
Even before the rollout begins, there should be a kickoff meeting that includes stakeholders such as data engineering, data science, and business users who will be impacted by the platform. Ideally, you've already achieved buy-in for data quality monitoring among the attendees, but this is another place to rally your team(s) around the cause and tie it back to business outcomes. It's also the stage in which you should share onboarding plans and timelines, hear concerns and wish lists, and show a demo of the platform.

Live training sessions
After the kickoff, you'll typically want to schedule one to three live training sessions for the following weeks. Sessions are usually mapped to teams since each organization within your business might have very different use cases and requirements. You should invite the employees who will be actively using the tool, especially those involved in configuration and setup. Depending on your build versus buy decision, the vendor or internal team that builds and manages the platform will host these sessions. (If working with a vendor, over time, you may build up enough in-house experience to be able to perform training on your own.)

Live trainings are sometimes accompanied by internal working sessions as needed for the teams to reconcile what they've learned and agree on data quality monitoring checks and configurations that address their specific needs.

On-demand curriculum
Especially for large companies with many teams to onboard, it can be very helpful to have access to an on-demand training curriculum, which may be a combination of written tutorials and video walkthroughs to accommodate different learning styles. This allows users to proceed at their own pace and gives

them additional resources for topics that would be difficult to scale through live trainings.

Office hours

During the onboarding phase, and even beyond it, many teams find it helpful to have the option of attending a weekly office hours with the vendor/responsible internal team. This allows users to discuss any issues in person with someone who is an expert on the data quality monitoring platform. To facilitate learning, these discussions can be recorded and shared.

Ongoing support

Whether coming from the internal team that maintains the platform or the external vendor, there should be someone responsible for proactive support on an ongoing basis. This might include a dedicated Slack channel for direct access to platform experts as well as regular sessions to review the platform road map and feature updates (regular release notes should also be made available to users). Whoever is supporting the platform should establish monitoring for errors, performance, and infrastructure issues, as well as target SLAs for resolution (e.g., resolve P1 issues in one hour).

Onboarding, training, and support are ultimately not just a way to reduce friction; they're a way to improve engagement with data quality at your organization. They help evangelize the platform and circulate it internally, identifying connections and opportunities to use the monitoring solution on tangential teams that might not have even been part of the initial needs assessment. The best practices above also mitigate the common problem of people failing silently and giving up on trying to use the tool at all.

Improving Data Quality Over Time

Ultimately, you are investing in data quality monitoring because you want to improve data quality at your organization. While having a great data quality monitoring platform is a starting point, it's also not the entire story. There are a few strategies that you can take to ensure that your organization is continually improving and create a culture that is truly invested in data quality from day one.

Initiatives

You will need to identify and commit to data health initiatives that go beyond any single tool or interface and make changes to the way that you work with data.

Examples include:

- Conducting an audit of third-party data sources. Which ones are in use at your business? Which ones are being monitored?

- Investing in additional data infrastructure that integrates with your data quality monitoring tool, such as a data catalog.

- Creating documentation, such as runbooks, for debugging issues. This reduces the problem of siloed knowledge that only lives with a certain team or individual (and will be lost when people change teams or leave the company).

- Ensuring there is an owner for each table with clear notification channels and a triage process, as described in Chapter 6.

- Developing contracts between data producers and data consumers that align expectations about the data (e.g., what constitutes late delivery, or who is notified when data is updated).

We find that data health often builds momentum at an organization as a result of investing in data quality monitoring in the first place—sort of like how making that first move to invest in your health, such as committing to regular exercise, can kick off all kinds of related changes, like eating a more nutritious diet.

Metrics

When you are investing in improving your data quality, you'll most likely be interested in ways to measure your progress. This can be important for many different reasons, whether it's helping encourage other teams to use your tool or demonstrating impact to senior leadership.

Triage and resolution

One of the most important metrics for success is not just the number of data quality issues detected, but the magnitude of those issues and *how quickly they were resolved*. Being committed to triaging and resolving issues is going to make or break the return value of your monitoring investment.

To this end, it's essential to have a clear process around what to do when a data quality issue is detected and continue to hone and iterate on this process. Institute SLAs on response times for data quality issues and ensure that they are communicated clearly across teams.

Executive dashboards

Senior leadership often benefits from a dashboard of high-level metrics about the data quality platform. This might include the level of monitoring coverage across the warehouse, week-over-week trends in the number of issues detected, or the tables with the most issues. Refer back to Chapter 3 for more dashboard visuals and details.

Scorecards

Another way to track progress on data quality initiatives is to give each table a data quality scorecard that combines different aspects of the table's health into a single value, percentage, or grade.

As an example, to assemble a table's scorecard, each time you run data quality monitoring on that table, you could give points for checks that pass and deduct points for checks that fail. You would probably want to assign each data quality check a weight, since not all checks will be equally important. One way to do this would be to use the check's priority level (high, normal, or low, from Chapter 6), so high-priority checks have the greatest impact on the overall data quality score for the table.

Scorecards provide an at-a-glance view of a table's data quality and allow you to compare tables quickly. When tables can be linked to organizational information, scorecards become a way to understand which teams, business units, or data warehouses are improving data quality and which are falling behind. For all these reasons, scorecards can be very effective not only within the monitoring platform but also when integrated with other systems such as data catalogs.

In assembling a scorecard, you'll often need to make tough product and UX decisions. For example, you might decide that a data quality score is more useful when divided into categories that explain where the table needs to improve, such as in Figure 8-1. However, decisions about what categories to define and how to classify checks into those categories are far from straightforward.

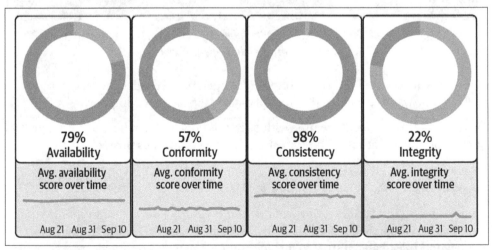

Figure 8-1. An example of a data quality scorecard where scores are given across four categories and tracked over time.

In practice, scorecards are rarely one-size-fits-all. At a minimum, a data quality platform should provide APIs or data exports that allow organizations to extract data needed to construct such scorecards. For example, a history of every check run, along with the priority of the check and tags associated with it and whether the check passed or failed, could be the basis of a simple scorecard. This data can also be consolidated with other data the organization has to build their own custom data governance dashboards.

From Chaos to Clarity

OpenAI. (2023). ChatGPT (September 25 Version) [Large language model]. https://chat.openai.com

Now that you're armed with the tools to solve operational challenges that arise, you're well on your way to changing the story of data quality at your company.

We're so glad you've spent the time with us in this book to learn how to automate data quality monitoring at scale. To recap, this journey has taken us through:

Chapter 1
    Why data quality matters and how mistakes affect your business

Chapter 2
    What a comprehensive data quality solution looks like, and why that must go beyond rules-based testing to include automation with machine learning

Chapter 3
    How to assess the ROI your business would get from such a solution

Chapter 4

An algorithm for automating data quality monitoring at scale with machine learning

Chapter 5

Tuning and testing your model to ensure it performs well on real-world data

Chapter 6

How to implement notifications and avoid the common pitfall of over-alerting

Chapter 7

Why and how to integrate your monitoring with other data tools and systems

Chapter 8

Deploying your solution, onboarding users, and continually improving data quality

Many businesses today are operating a data factory without sufficient quality control. Legacy methods are failing to grapple with the volumes of data that modern enterprises work with every day. Fortunately, as the rest of the data stack is modernizing, so is data quality monitoring. As we've seen in this book, automating data quality monitoring with machine learning is a powerful solution to proactively detect and explain issues that might be lurking deep in your most important data, affecting machine learning models, BI dashboards, and ultimately, the decisions that drive your bottom line.

We've shared openly in this book, including things Jeremy wished he'd known when Anomalo was first getting started, because we believe in democratizing data quality. We want more people who work with data, from practitioners fighting fires to senior leadership worried about building on an unstable foundation, to know that there is a path forward. It's a path that leads to higher morale, better business outcomes, and the knowledge that you can trust the data your company relies on. Now you're ready to take the next step.

Types of Data Quality Issues

This appendix presents additional information about the types of data quality issues that are commonly encountered in real-world data. This list is helpful to consider as you evaluate the data quality monitoring solution you are building or buying. Ultimately, you'll want to have a strategy for identifying and addressing each of these types of issues for each important dataset in your organization.

For each of these data quality issues, we will provide an example, a summary of common causes, an assessment of how these issues typically affect analytics (using data and humans to inform decisions) and machine learning (using data and algorithms to automate processes), and our recommendations for how best to monitor a data source for these issues.

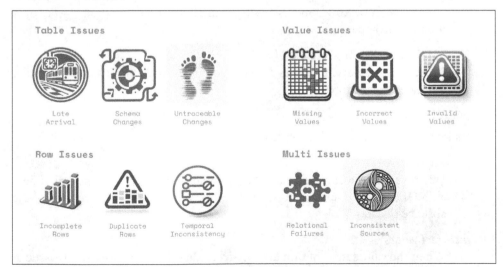

Figure A-1. Types of data quality issues organized into four categories (DALL-E 3)

As Figure A-1 shows, we have organized the issues in this appendix into four broad categories that indicate *at what level* the issues affect data.

- Table issues

  Issues that affect the entirety of the table, and aren't specific to individual rows or values:

  Late arrival
  > When data arrives late and is not available to a consuming system by the time the system needs the data

  Schema changes
  > When there are structural changes in the data such as new or dropped columns, changes in column names, changes in data types for columns, or changes in the JSON schema in semistructured columns

  Untraceable changes
  > When the records in a table are updated in place in ways that cannot be audited after the fact

- Row issues

  Issues affecting entire rows of data in the table:

  Incomplete rows
  > When data arrives, but only a fraction of the rows exist that ought to be there; usually, a specific segment of data is missing

  Duplicate rows
  > When the same row appears multiple times in the data when it was only intended to appear once

  Temporal inconsistency
  > When there are discrepancies or inconsistencies in the timing or sequencing of related data records

- Value issues

  Issues affecting specific values or cells of data:

  Missing values
  > When values in a column in a dataset are not populated, and instead appear as NULL, zero, empty strings, or other sentinel values that represent the absence of data

  Incorrect values
  > When the values in a column are incorrect, due to either a miscoding issue at a record level, or a structural error that misrepresents some or all records

Invalid values
> When values fail to conform to specified formats, constraints, or business rules

- Multi issues

Issues about how multiple tables relate to one another:

Relational failures
> When the relational integrity between two data sources fails for some records, leading to duplicate or missing joins

Inconsistent sources
> When there are differences in data values over time or across data sources that should otherwise be identical

Note that these issues aren't necessarily independent, as some of these can be both causes *and* symptoms of underlying issues, and so they may co-occur. For example, a source table may arrive late, which causes a relational failure in the transformation of the data, and missing data in a fact table.

We've tried to make this list as exhaustive as we can. But note that we explicitly excluded *semantic* issues, which might cover cases where data is technically correct but misunderstood by users, and *accessibility* issues, where again the data is correct but simply cannot be accessed. Both of these are important data governance issues that can be addressed with data catalogs and access control platforms.

Table Issues

Late Arrival

Definition

Data arrives late and is not available to a consuming system by the time the system needs the data.

Example

The system that moves a web application's event logs from S3 into a data warehouse stops processing new log records, such that there is no event data for the most recent day when analysts log in to view dashboards about user behavior.

Causes

- No data is being produced upstream, either at the point of capture (logging is not working) or because of a processing failure or outage in an upstream system or third party.

- A system responsible for loading data into a data warehouse is not working, either because of an outage or a fatal exception encountered in processing the data.

- A system responsible for transforming the data is not working, either because of an outage or a fatal failure in the logic of the transformation being applied (e.g., a SQL query begins to throw an exception in the warehouse).

- The pipeline producing the data stopped publishing because of other data quality issues upstream; late data is intended as an affordance to the end user that data for the current period is not ready to be consumed.

Analytics impact

- Dashboards usually appear to be broken when data is late—there may be visualizations that don't render, or that throw an error in the dashboard, or they may show NULL or 0 values.

- Users usually recognize that the data is gone and will come back to view the dashboard later. If this happens frequently, users will begin to lose confidence in the availability of the data and will seek out other sources or make decisions without data.

- Operational use cases such as analysis of current marketing campaigns or current site behavior will be disproportionately impacted by late data for the most recent period.

ML impact

- *Model training.* Often not disrupted by this, as model training usually takes place over a long history of data.

- *Model inference.* Late data often leads to ML features that are NULL or 0 when they should be some meaningful value instead. Or late data may mean that an ML model is using data that is out of date. In both cases, this introduces bias into the ML models that can cause predictions to vary wildly.

How to monitor

- One approach is to use table observability monitoring. On a regular schedule, collect the metadata for when the table was last updated. Then build a time series model to predict when the next update should arrive, and alert if the update arrives late. However, this might miss a case where the table is being updated in place, but new records still have not arrived; it might also miss when a table is dropped and replaced with no new records.

- The most robust approach is to query for the availability of records in the most recent time partition of the data. Observe how long it typically takes for records to arrive over time, and then again build a time series model to anticipate what time (or day) the records should arrive, and alert if that does not happen.

- Note that, instead of using time series models, you can also set a hard SLA for when the table should be updated, or when the data should arrive. This is advantageous in case you have users or systems that need the data to arrive by a specified time. But note that this will be difficult to maintain at scale.

Schema Changes

Definition

There are structural changes in the data such as new or dropped columns, changes in column names, changes in data types for columns, or changes in the JSON schema in semistructured columns.

Example

A column name is confusing, and so the engineering team decides to rename it to make it clearer. However, downstream data processing systems depend on that column name, and are not also changed, resulting in data processing failures (late or incomplete data) or missing data.

Causes

- The root cause of these changes is almost always an intentional change meant to expand, optimize, or refactor the data being captured at runtime.

- Production applications' data frameworks (e.g., Django) have robust mechanisms for ensuring these changes are propagated throughout the application (so-called "migrations"), but this will not extend to systems that are ingesting data emitted by these applications and must be accounted for manually.

- JSON-formatted data is prized for its flexibility—new data can be captured without having to perform migrations in the current system or in downstream applications. However, any downstream application that depends on the structure of that JSON data may be disrupted by those changes. They are often much more frequent and happen with less oversight.

Analytics impact

- In their simplest form, schema changes will make columns unavailable, and simply break the dashboards that depend on them.

- In more complex cases, a schema change is the root cause of what appears to be a missing data or distribution change—and so manifests in that manner.

ML impact

- *Model training.* When schemas change, it can be impossible to backfill historical data appropriately (e.g., if new information is being captured or the type changes in a way that is lossy). In these cases, ML models will become less powerful as their data is inconsistent over time.

- *Model inference.* If a schema change occurs and a model hasn't been retrained to account for it, then the model may simply fail (as the data is not in the correct format or shape for predictions), or it may make wild predictions as the changed data is forcefully converted to NULL or other sentinel or imputed values.

How to monitor

- Validation rules can be used to explicitly state what the schema ought to be for any given table. However, this is very hard to maintain over time.

- A more automated approach takes a snapshot of the schema data at some regular cadence (we do this daily at Anomalo) and automatically detects adverse changes, such as columns being dropped or renamed.

Untraceable Changes

Definition

The records in a table are updated in place in ways that cannot be audited after the fact.

Example

A digital advertising company only stores the current state of its campaigns. Campaigns are often extended, but there is no history of the original end dates since they keep getting overwritten. Reporting based on projected campaign end dates is unreliable. Although campaign start dates should not change, they can be overwritten as well. Campaigns can also be renamed while they are running. When analysts pull reports day-to-day, their numbers don't match and they cannot trace back to the reason why.

Causes

- Dimensional data is often updated in place to show the current status of customers or locations. Attributes of a location can change, such as if it is open or temporarily closed, or a customer can have a new address in a different state. If the time of these changes is not tracked, historical reports based on the current versions of dim tables may be incorrect.

- Customer transactional or claims data may be updated in place, with an initial record created when the transaction begins. Various fields will begin as NULL values because they are unknown (the final shipping date or the final amount of the claim, for example). Then, as these events become known, the records are updated. This leads to data that consistently has more NULL values for recent records.

- Data pipelines may be "rerun" to correct mistakes and previously identified issues without preserving a record of the incorrect data to compare to.

- Tables may have a data architecture where the entire table is truncated and reloaded on a daily basis, masking which records actually had changes.

- Note that some data warehouses support the notion of "time traveling" to review the history of a table at a recent point in time. This can help to mediate the impact of these issues, but support is typically limited to very recent time periods and may be difficult to scale to record level time travel for ML applications.

Analytics impact

- Data analysis on these tables is built on quicksand, since running the same query two days in a row does not provide the same results. The analyst is unable to recreate the conditions that created the prior day's run.

- Metrics for segments of data may have inconsistent values in reporting from one day to the next due to changing dimensional data, causing analysts to lose trust in the data.

- Historical analysis becomes impossible because the analyst cannot recreate the world as it was.

- Metrics computed over time may show sudden sharp movements in recent days or weeks due to recent data being incomplete, whereas older records have completed their updates.

ML impact

- *Model training.* Updating data in place without maintaining the full audit log of changes erases a lot of information that might be valuable signals for an ML model.

The worst-case scenario is that updates to historical data "leak" information about the response that the model is trying to predict. For example, if a customer table is updated every time an order is placed, then this data cannot be used to predict the chance that a customer will place another order in the future. If it is, then the presence of recent changes (or even more complete records) will be a very strong signal that the customer will make purchases in the past. But this will not generalize to future predictions.

- *Model inference.* Models are often trained on historical data that is fully matured (all in-place updates have been completed). This is acceptable, but only if the model will then be used to make predictions on data that is *also* fully mature. In practice, this is rarely the case, and the model will be used on data that is still incomplete, and the results of the model will be very biased.

How to monitor

- The only way to reliably detect this issue is to compare summary statistics or samples of data drawn from a given table for a specific set of records over time. The set of records could be a randomly chosen set of primary keys. Or it could be a specific time window as specified using a SQL WHERE clause querying for a date or time partition of data.

- Then, you can monitor for drift in the count of the number of rows over time (data is removed or added in place over time), or for drift in key statistics, like data quality or business metrics.

- A more robust approach repeatedly samples data from a given time partition over time and uses ML to detect differences in the distribution drift of that data. This can identify the specific columns and segments of data that are updated in place in a fully automated manner.

Row Issues

Incomplete Rows

Definition

Data arrives, but only a fraction of the rows exist that ought to be there. Usually, a specific segment of data is missing.

Example

All of the records for a given day of data have arrived except for the records from one country, which is delayed because it is processed by a third party in that country that is having an outage.

Causes

- Data may be collected via different processes or vendors for different segments. For example, data from different regions comes from different cloud availability zones. Or different types of events are collected using different instrumentation.

- Insofar as data is collected or processed separately by segment, then it is common for there to be a failure or delay in capture, transmission, or loading of data from just one or a handful of segments, but not all of them.

Analytics impact

- For any metric evaluated in the data, the missing segment may be above or below average for that metric—this will bias the metric up or down accordingly. For example, if revenue per transaction is lower in Android events, and they are missing, then overall revenue per transaction will appear higher than expected.

- When the metrics are biased in this way, they may lead teams to reach incorrect conclusions. For example, any recent business change may be "blamed" for the resulting metric change.

- The smaller the segment causing the data to be incomplete, the harder it is to diagnose the root cause of incompleteness. Biased metrics, as described here, may become the new normal.

- It may not be possible to backfill the incomplete data once the issue is identified, leading to a permanent scar in the data.

- Dashboards that show segment breakdowns for the metric may appear to be broken as a certain segment suddenly disappears in the dashboard, leading teams to disregard the dashboard as a reliable source of truth.

ML impact

- *Model training.* In rare situations, a segment of data can go missing and undetected for a long period of time. In these cases, the data would be absent from the training dataset, and the model would be unable to learn how to behave for that segment of data. Then, when the model is used to make predictions on records from that segment of data, they may be very unreliable.

- *Model inference.* If records are not being processed for a segment at prediction time, then those predictions will not be available for the business to act on. This may lead to default impersonalized behavior for consumers or failover to rules-based behavior for decisioning systems, which will all underperform.

How to monitor

- Table observability methods can be used to monitor for incomplete rows; however, since metadata is being used, they will only be able to detect changes in the *overall* row count for the table and will not be nearly as sensitive to the specific row counts added for a time partition.

- A more robust approach is to count the rows for time partitions (days or hours) using a SQL query and a partition time column in the table. Then you can use a time series model to detect if there is an unexpected drop in table row counts.

- Unsupervised ML models are very good at detecting if there is a specific segment of data that has disappeared or become much less common than expected in the data.

- For very high cardinality segments of data (e.g., store POS systems), explicitly confirming all stores are included via joining to a dimensional table of stores may be necessary.

Duplicate Rows

Definition

The same row appears multiple times in the data when it was only intended to appear once.

Example

A credit card payment transaction dataset is joined to a reference table of metadata available for each type of payment transaction. The reference dataset is maintained by hand in Excel and occasionally dropped and reloaded when there are changes. A mistake is made, and a payment type is added a second time instead of being edited in place. This data is loaded, and now all of the credit payment transactions for that type are joined to two reference records, causing thousands of transactions to be duplicated downstream.

Causes

- As illustrated in the credit card example, a small change that introduces one duplicate record in a single table may propagate into a large number of duplicates once the data is joined to other tables. So, duplicate data tends to proliferate and can even expand exponentially if a table with duplicate data is joined to itself (to match some rows or the table with others, say, over time).

- One common cause of duplicates is when the same records are loaded into a data warehouse multiple times. This can happen when there is an outage in the system loading the data, and a data engineer has to manually resume the loading operations. The same file, or parts of it, may be inadvertently loaded twice.

- Duplicate data can also arise from logging in distributed systems. These systems are meant to be very tolerant to failures of individual nodes. And so they often guarantee "at least once" execution of tasks. However, that means it is possible they can run more than once, due to communication issues in the distributed system. The result can then be duplicated records (possibly with different timestamps).

Analytics impact

- Duplicate data will tend to lead to overstatements of analytical results—counts of records will be higher than expected, as will any sum-based statistics. This can appear to inflate the performance of a business, or of any entity that you are aggregating over.
- Duplicate data can also bias any average statistics, as the records that are duplicated will effectively be given more weight in comparison to the records that are not duplicated.

ML impact

- *Model training.*
  - When data is duplicated at random in just the training data (a rare occurrence), then it is unlikely to materially bias the result of the model. In fact, many algorithms use random sampling of rows, which will not be affected at all by randomly duplicating the data first.
  - However, if there is bias in the duplicated data, then the model will learn to pay more attention to these duplicated records. And in extreme cases, it will memorize them (since they appear so often) and have an unreasonably high confidence in its predictions.
  - The worst (and most common) case is when data is duplicated before training and testing splits are done. This will result in some records appearing in both the training data and the test data (since they appear twice, this will be possible some fraction of the time). This kind of "leakage" of records from the training data to the test data will lead to invalid estimates of the model performance. This can cause the process of training the model to select a model that is inappropriate for the data, resulting in performance in production that is far inferior to the performance experienced when developing the model.

- *Model inference.*

  — Duplicate data at inference time is not inherently problematic for the ML model. However, whatever system is consuming the predictions of the model will have to contend with duplicate records.

  — Often this means that the decision system will try to make the same decision multiple times per entity. This could lead to duplicate emails being sent, duplicate coupons being given, duplicate loan applications being created, etc.

How to monitor

- Duplicate rows can be detected by creating a validation rule that ensures that the data is unique on a primary key column, or on a combination of columns that define a primary key. However, this requires asking subject matter experts to test and define this rule for every table of interest.

- A more scalable approach is to automatically identify columns that are consistently unique over time, and alert if duplicate values appear unexpectedly in any of these columns.

Temporal Inconsistency

Definition

There are discrepancies or inconsistencies in the timing or sequencing of related data records.

Example

A marketing team is analyzing the sequence of steps that users take when they first visit the site. There are key events that are tracked, which include the first page the user visits, when they create their account, when they first add an item to their cart, and when they first complete a transaction. However, one of the distributed systems that is logging events related to adding items to carts is experiencing degraded performance, and so it has built up a long queue of cart additions to log. The timestamp captured is the moment the log record is written, rather than when the item was added to the cart in the user's browser. The result is that the first item added is sometimes *after* the first completed transaction. The analysis excludes these records as invalid, and it reduces the computed percentage of users who transact, given they have added an item to their cart.

Causes

- The most common cause of these issues is that the timestamps for events are either incorrect or the wrong timestamp is being used (in the example above, we are using the logged timestamp rather than the client-side event timestamp).
- Another very common cause of these issues is that different columns in the same table are stored with "wall times" in different time zones. For example, a record update timestamp is stored in coordinated universal time (UTC), but a transaction time is stored in the local time where the transaction occurred.
- These kinds of temporal issues can also often creep into downstream transformations of data due to logical mistakes in SQL. For example, an analytics engineer might accidentally take the maximum time an item was added to the cart in the first session, rather than the minimum. For users who transacted multiple times in their first session, this would also lead to add-to-cart times that are later than the transaction time.

Analytics impact

- When the temporal sequence of events is inaccurate, then computations about the time it takes for events to occur are biased. This can cause analytical errors in the estimates of how long key activities take to complete. Time is money, as they say, and so these inaccuracies can lead to suboptimal or even value-destroying decisions.
- In some cases, the sequence of events becomes impossible (a user checks out without adding anything to their cart). If these impossible records are removed, then the results are biased by their absence.
- If they are included, then they can have wild consequences. For example, we have seen issues with timestamp conversion that have caused events to be far, far in the future. When times for these events are computed and averaged with other times, they can completely overwhelm the computation and lead to irrational conclusions.

ML impact

- *Model training.*
  - The time it takes for events to occur can be a very important signal to an ML model (how long a customer takes to complete an action or how long an internal process takes). These inaccuracies will tend to bias the model to think these events are less important than they really are.
  - The more problematic case is when the events themselves are a part of what you are trying to predict. For example, if you are predicting how long it

will take for a delivery to be made and this measure is biased by incorrect temporal data, then your entire model can be biased and it will perform poorly in production.

- *Model inference.* At prediction time, these temporal inconsistencies will appear as incorrect values, which will have the same adverse effects as for other incorrect string or numeric types of data.

How to monitor

- Complex validation rules can be created that self-join the table to itself, compute the sequence or interarrival time between events, and then set explicit guards around the ordering of sequences or what the arrival times between events should be.

- Unsupervised ML algorithms can detect some of these issues, insofar as the data is reshaped to have one row per entity or transaction, with the sequence of events and timestamps appearing as multiple columns. The algorithm will be able to learn the relationships between these columns and identify if there are unexpected changes.

Value Issues

Missing Values

Definition

Values in a column in a dataset are not populated, and instead appear as NULL, zero, empty strings, or other sentinel values that represent the absence of data.

Example

In an auto insurance dataset, there is a column for each insurance policy that shows how many doors there are in the vehicle being insured. There are valid reasons for this column to be NULL (e.g., doors are not relevant for motorcycles), but suddenly the percentage of NULL values increases because a third-party source of vehicle information is incomplete, causing a left join to fail, which introduces NULL values for cars that should have a door number. NULL can become an overloaded concept in a database: it can represent that the value is not appropriate (motorcycles have no doors), unknown (the vehicle type is not yet known), or missing (the car is known but the number of doors field is still missing).

Causes

- Missing data can appear at the point of collection when the event itself is captured (e.g., a record is written), but a measurement about the event (e.g., context for the event, or key outcomes) is not captured.

- Missing data can also creep into data as it is moved from one system to another—for example, if a system that the data is being loaded into expects an alternate data type, then values may be coerced into the new data type, and values that cannot be coerced may become missing.

- Missing data is also often introduced via left joins. For example, when a set of transactions is left-joined to a dimension table, and there are join keys that are not present in the dimension table, then any data brought from the dimension table to the transactions will be missing for those keys.

- Missing data can also accumulate, where a small fraction of missing data at a granular level can turn into a larger fraction of missing data at an aggregate level. For example, in some platforms, if you compute the sum of a column that contains missing values, the result of the sum can be missing. Thus, a dataset that is only 1% missing at the transaction level can become 10% or 50% missing when aggregated by customer, product, or geography.

Analytics impact

- Missing data often biases analytics results. The most common treatment is that missing data is removed from the analysis. If the data is missing at random, then the results will just have more noise.

- But most data doesn't go missing at random; it goes missing for a specific reason. And usually the records that are missing are correlated to other segments of the dataset, which may have significantly higher or lower values for any metrics under analysis. This will cause a downward or upward bias in the analysis that can influence decisions.

ML impact

- *Model training.*
  - Missing raw data will often translate into ML features that are missing or have increases in default values (such as 0).
  - In some cases, a feature will become much less important to the model because it can only be used on a small percentage of observations. This will limit how powerful the model can be, as it won't be able to learn as much from this feature as it should be able to.

— In extreme cases, the missingness will be linked to the response outcome, due to a quirk in how the missingness was introduced. For example, a SQL bug causes a field to become missing only if a user has churned. Then, using this field in a model to predict churn will trick the model into thinking that missingness causes churn. This will make the model very untrustworthy at prediction time.

— Finally, the missingness can appear in the response itself (we don't know the outcome we are trying to predict). This will cause that data to be removed entirely from the modeling exercise, which will limit the strength of the model and bias its predictions on any records in the future that previously had this missingness pattern.

- *Model inference.*

— At prediction time, when a model is fed missing data that it doesn't expect, these missing values may cause the model to fail to make predictions entirely, which stops the system from functioning. To avoid that, missing values are often coerced into numeric values (often 0), which can lead to wildly inaccurate predictions if that value is not frequently present in the training data or is present in very different circumstances.

— In other cases, the missing values will be handled by the model gracefully (e.g., tree-based models can just integrate over splits on that feature), but if the values are missing for reasons that are different from how they were missing in the training data, the predictions will still be biased.

How to monitor

- Validation rules can be used to detect if data is missing, and metrics can be used to monitor the percentage of data that is missing. However, both require significant maintenance and care.

- Unsupervised ML is very effective at detecting if there is a sudden increase in missing data.

Incorrect Values

Definition

Values in a column are incorrect due to either a miscoding issue at a record level or a structural error that misrepresents some or all records.

Example

A social media platform is tracking the percentage of users who are taking specific actions (e.g., liking, sharing, or replying to content). The specific actions are tagged by the application code, and to facilitate more fine-grained analysis of user behavior, the application splits a tag in two to capture some finer nuance of the behavior (e.g., "shared" now becomes "shared with comment" or "shared directly"). However, this change is not clearly communicated to all downstream users, so some queries that are looking for the old, aggregated tag begin returning no records for recent periods of data.

Causes

- The most obvious cause of incorrect values is when they are captured incorrectly at the point of data entry—typically when a human is entering data into a form, and there are insufficient controls on that form. For example, a user may enter an address that is invalid or incorrect. In general, these issues are becoming less frequent, as there are better methods of input validation in modern applications. However, discrepancies can remain across systems, and master data management (MDM) tools can be used to master and reconcile information of this type.

- A more systemic cause of incorrect values is when the system generating the data (the application or the third party) makes a change in how the data is generated, logged, or processed that affects the values for specific records. Records that would have been represented by a specific string value in the past now have a new string value, or their numeric value has changed in a way that isn't related to the quantity being measured.

- In some cases, these changes are "bugs" that are misrepresenting the data and can be fixed in upstream systems. But in other cases they are intentional changes that may refine the granularity or units of the data being captured. For example, a financial transaction value might change from USD to EUR. Or a product dimension might change from being measured in inches to centimeters.

- Incorrect values can also enter into datasets due to changes in how the data is being processed. For example, SQL may be used to transform a dataset inside a data warehouse. That SQL will need to change periodically to accommodate new features in the input data, new requirements for the output of the SQL, or to adapt to other upstream changes. Each change in the SQL can introduce the risk of invalid values, such as when a mistake is made in a CASE WHEN statement that incorrectly reclassifies string values.

Analytics impact

- When values are incorrectly coded for individual records, there is unlikely to be a significant impact on analytics, which tend to use the data in aggregate. However, when a large percentage of values are incorrect, then statistics or visualizations based on that data can become badly biased.

- For example, many analytical queries will be narrowly focused on segments of data and will use WHERE SQL clauses to narrow the computation to a subset of rows. When values are incorrect, these SQL queries will miss the data entirely, or will include it in places where it should not be included. This can lead to large changes in volume and statistics insofar as these subsets differ from the norm (which they usually do).

- When numerical values are incorrect, then all of the analytical computations of these values are also inherently flawed. Computing sums, means, or other statistics will all be biased in proportion to the percentage of records and amount of variance introduced by the incorrect coding.

ML impact

- *Model training.*
  - When values are invalid, the ML model will still attempt to learn the relationship between the invalid values and the outcome that it is trying to predict. In the best-case scenario, there is no relationship, and the data simply isn't as useful as it could be, so the model's performance will be lower than it could have been (potentially causing false positives or false negatives).
  - But if the variable is an important one, then the invalid values will almost certainly affect the relationships the model learns between the outcome and the data. This can cause the model to associate values with an outcome that is not real. As soon as the data quality issue is fixed, the model will begin to behave very erratically.

- *Model inference.*
  - Whenever a model is presented with an incorrect value, this will affect the prediction of the model. The magnitude of the prediction will depend on how important the affected data is to the model (how much "weight" that data is given when making predictions), and the magnitude of the error in the coding of the data (where magnitude here is really measured in terms of how different the predictions become for affected records).
  - In practice, this can range from negligible (a small change in the precision of a floating point may not have a meaningful effect, or the miscoding of a category that isn't important to the model's prediction may have no effect), or it can completely ruin the predictions for affected records, causing wildly erroneous decisions to made.

How to monitor

- Validation rules can encode a user's expectations for what types of values in a given column are correct given other data in the column, but this requires a great deal of care and maintenance.

- Time series models can be used to monitor the percentage of records available for each common value in a column and can detect if there is an unexpected drift. However, this approach is best used with just a handful of critical columns on important tables. And it will not be able to handle columns with numeric, time, or other high cardinality values.

- Unsupervised ML models are very good at detecting unexpected changes in the distribution of the data caused by incorrect values, insofar as these changes are affecting a meaningful percentage of the rows.

Invalid Values

Definition

Values fail to conform to specified formats, constraints, or business rules.

Example

A mainframe system of customer information exports dates in a YYYYMMDD string format. This data is loaded into Snowflake, where marketing campaigns are configured to send customers emails based on their date of birth. A configuration change is made in the mainframe, and now the dates are exported in DDMMYYYY format instead. In Snowflake, this results in birthdates that are far in the distant past, resulting in users whose age ranges are never selected for marketing campaigns, causing a significant drop in marketing activity and new customer acquisition.

Causes

- Many data format issues are caught early in data extraction and loading, as the type of the data is inconsistent with the type of the table it is being loaded into. For example, a string-formatted integer would throw an error in a data load into a table that expected the date to be formatted as a numeric type.

- But, within the format constraints of the column, it is still possible that the format of the values is inconsistent with what users or downstream systems might expect. This is most common with string columns, which, aside from requiring valid character sets and possibly having limits on length, rarely have any other types enforced. It is also common to have incorrect formats in JSON or other nested data (see Chapter 3 for more on these types).

- Format issues are most common when changes to the systems capturing or logging the data itself change, causing the format to suddenly change. As an example, a third party might decide to begin representing US phone numbers in (XXX) XXX-XXXX format instead of in XXX-XXX-XXXX format.

- In other cases, format issues are caused by there being inconsistent standards for the format within the same enterprise. These inconsistencies may not matter when data is stored and processed separately in each organization. But as soon as the data is brought together in a single data warehouse or data lake, these format issues can wreak havoc on data users.

- Finally, there can be invalid data that doesn't meet constraints that the business has in place. For example, it may not be possible for there to be a negative monetary transaction (where the company owes the customer for buying the product). In these cases, the issue is more that the data itself is incorrect, and it just may be more obvious than other incorrect values because the value itself is not allowed.

Analytics impact

- Incorrect or inconsistently formatted data creates a significant drag on analytics teams, as they have to rectify these formatting issues if they want to join, union, or aggregate the data in consistent ways. This may need to be done on an ad hoc basis, significantly slowing down the time to produce analyses and insights.

- In other cases, when the data is simply invalid, the effect is the same as other invalid data, it may just be more obvious to the end user.

ML impact

- *Model training.*
  - High cardinality string data is not often directly used as an input into ML models, unless they are doing natural language processing on the data, which can in many cases be robust to variances in format.

  - However, if there is feature engineering happening on this data, inconsistently formatted data can hurt the model's ability to generalize across the differently formatted segments of the population of data it is trained upon. Typically this is discovered by the engineer who is doing the feature engineering, and like the analytics team, they simply have to do more work to overcome it.

- *Model inference.*
  - When the format of a string column changes unexpectedly, the features that are computed from that column may also change, which will cause a sudden shock to the ML model and will cause predictions to behave erratically.

How to monitor

- Invalid values can be found using validation rules, where a subject matter expert expresses the expected format of the data.

- Unsupervised ML can detect changes in value formats, especially if it can use pattern recognition in string values as an input into the ML model.

- Invalid values often cause downstream SQL to error due to type conversion issues which make them hard to monitor directly; validation rules using TRY_CAST can help catch these errors explicitly on an upstream form of the table where all column types are treated as variants.

Multi Issues

Relational Failures

Definition

The relational integrity between two data sources fails for some records, leading to duplicate or missing joins.

Example

An ecommerce company wants to analyze what marketing channels are driving the most order volume. A table containing marketing attribution data is left joined to another table that has customer order information. However, the customer attribution data is missing all customers whose first engagement was on Android due to an upstream logging issue. The result is that many of the orders are dropped, and none of the results include Android data.

Causes

- The most common causes of relational failures are actually other data quality issues—data in one of the tables that are being joined is either missing or duplicated, causing the join to fail to be one-to-one, or to produce more or fewer records per joined key than expected.

- A more subtle cause of relational failures is when the IDs that are used themselves have data quality issues, which could be incompatible formats, or incorrect values. For example, a user's email address might be hashed to an alphanumeric string to protect their privacy, but still provide a consistent way of identifying the user. If one source begins using a different hashing algorithm from the others, then the join will fail spectacularly.

- Finally, in some cases the join is logically incorrect. For example, if two tables are being joined on a day of month column, but one source is using the calendar day of month, whereas the other source is using the bank business day of month, the join will fail (there are more calendar days than business days in every month, so records will be lost).

Analytics impact

- The net result of relational failures is usually either incomplete rows (records are dropped), missing values (a left join leads to NULL values), or duplicate rows (a join is not one-to-one, and so there are Cartesian joins that explode the row counts). The impact on the analytics is the same as for these other data quality issues.

ML impact

- *Model training.* The impact will vary based on the net impact of the join failure (see the sections "Incomplete Rows", "Missing Values", or "Duplicate Rows").
- *Model inference.* The impact will vary based on the net impact of the join failure(see the sections "Incomplete Rows", "Missing Values", or "Duplicate Rows").

How to monitor

- Validation rules that express the expected join semantics between two tables can be used to monitor for adherence to those join semantics (at least one record, exactly one record, or one or more record as the result of a join).
- In other cases, these issues can be caught by unsupervised ML models in tables or views that are the result of joins on tables with relational issues.

Inconsistent Sources

Definition

There are differences in data values over time or across data sources that should otherwise be identical.

Example

A complex set of financial data is transformed, joined, aggregated, and summarized inside of a source relational database to produce internal financial metrics. The same raw data is exported from this source database, loaded into a cloud data warehouse, and then put through a similar set of transformations and aggregations, to produce what ought to be identical sets of reports that will be distributed to management and investors. However, there are discrepancies in key financial figures between the internal tools built on the source relational data and the external reports being generated by the warehouse.

Causes

- When the same data is processed in different ways, or through different systems, there can be data quality issues introduced into one data processing path that are absent in the other path. This can manifest as discrepancies in aggregates produced at the end of the pipeline.

- There can also be logical inconsistencies that are introduced in the two paths via code that is written in different languages, by different teams, or by the same team at different times. These inconsistencies will eventually show up in the data itself.

Analytics impact

- When data that ought to be the same is inconsistent, this usually means that one or both of the datasets are also of poor quality. Any of the other data quality issues we have discussed may be occurring in the raw, interim, or final datasets. These will lead to incorrect decisions and invalid insights in analytics based on any of this data.

- In some cases, the inconsistencies may be too small to have a meaningful impact on decisions. However, it is common for these inconsistencies to reduce the trust that end users have in the data, as they will manually try to reconcile individual statistics, and will question the integrity of the data or its processing if they find discrepancies.

ML impact

- *Model training.* The biggest ML impact is when the training data used to build the model is inconsistent with the data being used at inference time. This can often happen when ML engineers construct training datasets using historical data stored in a data warehouse or data lake. When a model built on that data is put into production, it may instead receive data coming in real time from the source systems. That data may be inconsistent with the raw data the original model was trained upon, which can lead to very poor performance of the ML model in production.

- *Model inference.* See the answer above for model training, as the primary issue here is inconsistency between data used in training and inference.

How to monitor

- Validation rules can be used to compute summary statistics for each table and to compare those summary statistics across sources. These statistics can also be segmented by time or business segment.

- Unsupervised ML can also be used to compare random samples of records drawn from both sources and can summarize the variances in the distribution and relationship of values.

- Finally, you can compare records one-by-one between two sources, but this is often very computationally expensive, as each record must be moved from each source to a third platform, which then compares the records in memory. This also requires identifying a primary key for each source such that the records can be joined together efficiently.

- Last but not least, if you can sort the data in a deterministic manner, then you can compute cryptographic hashes of the data, and compare those hash values. However, this is also very computationally expensive and will not give clear insight into exactly where the differences are, or how significant they are. The values themselves will also have to be identical, and be converted into string values in identical ways, which is very challenging to do across disparate platforms.

Index

About the Authors

Jeremy Stanley is cofounder and CTO at Anomalo. Prior to Anomalo, Jeremy was the VP of Data Science at Instacart, where he led machine learning and drove multiple initiatives to improve the company's profitability. Previously, he led data science and engineering at other hypergrowth companies like Sailthru and Collective. He has applied machine learning and AI technologies to everything from insurance and accounting to ad tech and last-mile delivery logistics. He's also a recognized thought leader in the data science community with hugely popular blog posts like "Deep Learning with Emojis (Not Math)" (*https://oreil.ly/LeYsD*). Jeremy holds a BS in mathematics from Wichita State University and an MBA from Columbia University. You can find Jeremy on LinkedIn (*https://www.linkedin.com/in/jeremystanley*) and on X (formerly known as Twitter) (*https://www.x.com/jeremystan*).

Paige Schwartz is a professional technical writer at Anomalo who has written for clients such as Airbnb, Grammarly, and OpenAI. She specializes in communicating complex software engineering topics to a general audience and has spent her career working with machine learning and data systems, including five years as a product manager on Google Search. She holds a joint BA in computer science and English from UC Berkeley.

Colophon

The animal on the cover of *Automating Data Quality Monitoring* is a basking shark (*Cetorhinus maximus*). Basking sharks are the second-largest fish, and while they may appear intimidating, they are generally harmless creatures.

Basking sharks can grow up to 12 meters and weigh up to 6 tons, and their large dorsal fin makes them easy to spot as they swim at the surface. They have a bulbous snout, and their heads are almost entirely encircled by gill slits. They feed by swimming slowly with their jaws open wide, catching zooplankton in rows of finger-like structures called gill rakers. Over an hour, a basking shark can filter approximately 2,000 tons of water for food. They can be found worldwide in temperate latitudes.

Basking sharks have been hunted to the point of being endangered. Despite protections on them, they are still caught in bycatch or get entangled in fishing gear. They are also at risk of being struck and killed by boats. Many of the animals on O'Reilly covers are endangered; all of them are important to the world.

The cover illustration is by Karen Montgomery, based on an antique line engraving from *English Cyclopedia*. The series design is by Edie Freedman, Ellie Volckhausen, and Karen Montgomery. The cover fonts are Gilroy Semibold and Guardian Sans. The text font is Adobe Minion Pro; the heading font is Adobe Myriad Condensed; and the code font is Dalton Maag's Ubuntu Mono.

Printed in the USA
CPSIA information can be obtained
at www.ICGtesting.com
JSHW062150050224
56676JS00012B/182

9 781098 145934